MY "SOLDIER" BOY

COMEDY-FARCE IN THREE ACTS

BY

ALFRED MALTBY AND FRANK LINDO

―――――

LONDON
SAMUEL FRENCH, LTD.
PUBLISHERS
89 STRAND

NEW YORK
SAMUEL FRENCH
PUBLISHER
26 W. 22D STREET

MY "SOLDIER" BOY.

Produced at the Criterion Theatre, London, on the 3d of
January, 1899.

CAST.

MONTAGUE MENDLE . . .	Mr. Weedon Grossmith.
JONAS TODDENHAM . . .	Mr. Alfred Maltby.
COLONEL ROSCOE	Mr. Ivan Watson.
CAPTAIN CULLENDAR . . .	Mr. Roper Spyers.
LIEUTENANT ALLISON . .	Mr. Charles Garth.
MICHAEL O'DOCHERTY . .	Mr. A. E. George.
LYDIA MENDLE	Miss Ellis Jeffreys.
MRS. MORRISON	Miss Helen Ferrers.
GERALDINE	Miss Margaret Halstan.
MARTHA	Miss Jennie M'Nulty.

MY " SOLDIER " BOY.

CHARACTERS.

MONTAGUE MENDLE . . . . *A Solicitor.*
CAPTAIN CECIL CULLENDAR . ⎫
ARCHIE ALLISON . . . . . ⎬ *12th Hussars.*
COLONEL ROSCOE . . . . . ⎭
JONAS TODDENHAM . . . . *Mendle's Stepfather.*
MICHAEL O'DOCHERTY . . .
LYDIA MENDLE . . . . . .
MRS. MORRISON . . . . *A business-like Woman.*
GERALDINE MORRISON . . .
MARTHA . . . .

ACT I.

DECEPTION.

Scene . . . . Mendle's rooms.

ACT II.

EVICTION.

Scene . . . . In Barracks.

ACT III.

DETECTION.

Scene . . . . Same as Act I.

PROPERTY PLOT.

ACT I.—SITTING-ROOM.

Comfortably furnished, half lawyer's office. Small table down R. Small table R. C. with cover, chair each side, some cut flowers on it. Curtain to D. R. 1 E. Fireplace R. 2 E., overmantel, clock, vases, 2 glass vases for cut flowers, fender, fire-irons, hearthrug, fire screen or plants, armchair by fire, cushion on armchair. Curtains and fancy blind to draw up and down to window C. Small table with bowl and plant under window. Small sideboard C. with drawer, spirit tantalus with colored water, knife and fork, small tablecloth, small cruet, plate, napkin, half-a-dozen wine glasses, all on sideboard. Chart up L. C. Curtains to opening L. C. Small table with plant in bowl at back L. C. Large picture on flat at back. Office knee table with drawers down L., writing materials, hand bell, stationery rack, briefs, blotting pad Revolving office chair L. Chart L. C. Rugs to all doors, Cabinet with china up L. Curtain to door L. 2 E. Carpet. Two electric bell presses, 1 E. L. and R.

HAND PROPERTIES OFF STAGE.—Tray, cup and saucer, silver teapot and tea, milk in jug, sugar basin and lump sugar, toast rack and toast, silver cutlet dish with property cutlet. Six letters for Martha. Salver, 2 ladies' cards, 1 gentleman's card. Written letter for Martha. Letter for Mike. Door bell for Prompter.

ACT II.—ANTE-ROOM IN BARRACKS.

Six bent wood chairs. Bent wood armchair. Sofa. Fireplace R. 2 E., fender, fire-irons, fire screen, hearthrug. Small table up C. Writing cabinet L., writing materials. Table L. C., box of cigarettes, match stand, and ash tray on it. Kurd rugs to all doors. Sporting prints, trophies, shields, lances, boxing gloves, foils, fencing masks. Plenty of photographs on the scene. Curtains to window. Swords, leather and burnisher, 2 cigar boxes, 2 gas brackets, ram's head and cup on table up C. Two flint lock pistols hanging on flat L.

HAND PROPERTIES OFF STAGE.—Salver and brandy bottle, and syphon of soda and tumbler off R. 1 E. Letter on salver off L. C. Taper and match off L. C. Hand bell off L. I E. Stone and cocoanut shells for clatter of horses' hoofs, and rattle of chains off L. Bank notes for Toddenham. Bugler for trumpet calls stationed off L.

ACT III.—SAME AS ACT I.

Candlestick with glass shade, candle lighted off L. C. Wood and glass crash off L. Bandages and broom off R. I E. Police notice for Martha. Torn letter for Toddenham.

GAS AND LIME PLOT.

ACT I.

Full up ; lengths to all doors.
Amber lime behind window.

ACT II.

Full up ; lengths behind all doors.
Amber lime behind window ; change to red at cue.
Take lime off at cue.
Lower battens to half ; full up at cue.
Two single gas brackets on C. flats (to light).
If perforated back cloth of barrack yard ; bunch behind it.

ACT III.

Battens and floats three-quarters down ; full up at cue.
Amber lime behind window.
Lengths to doors.

SCENE PLOT.

ACTS I. AND III.—COMFORTABLE SITTING-ROOM.

Street backing.   Interior backing.

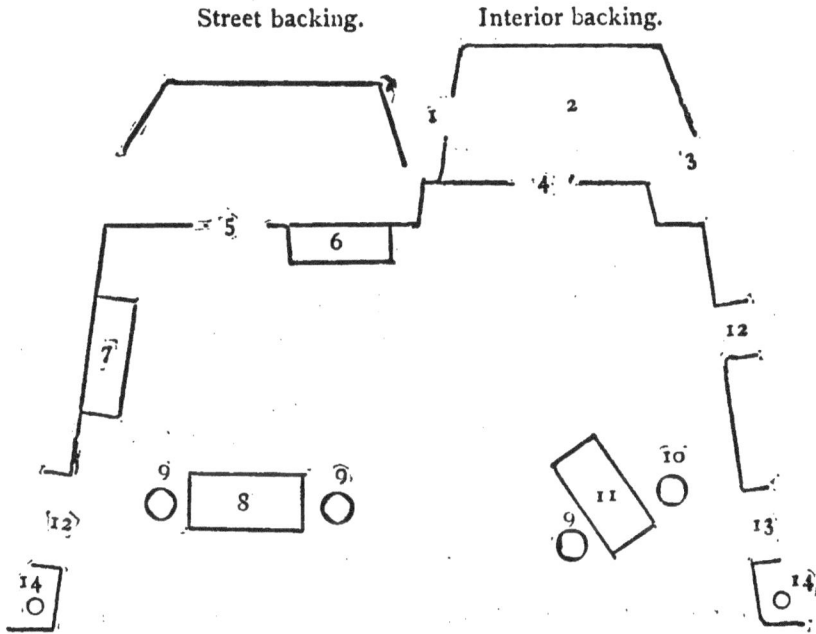

1. Street door: 2. Hall; 3. Opening into house; 4. Opening; 5. Sash window; 6. Sideboard; 7. Fireplace; 8. Table; 9. Chairs; 10. Office chair; 11. Office table; 12. Door with lock and key; 13. Green baize door, brass nail panels, lock and key, if possible; 14. Electric bell presses.

Carpet to cover stage.

ACT II.—ANTEROOM IN BARRACKS, QUITE PLAIN CHAMBER.

Exterior of barracks and yard.   Corridor backing.

There must be plenty of room to pass this window and on to opening.

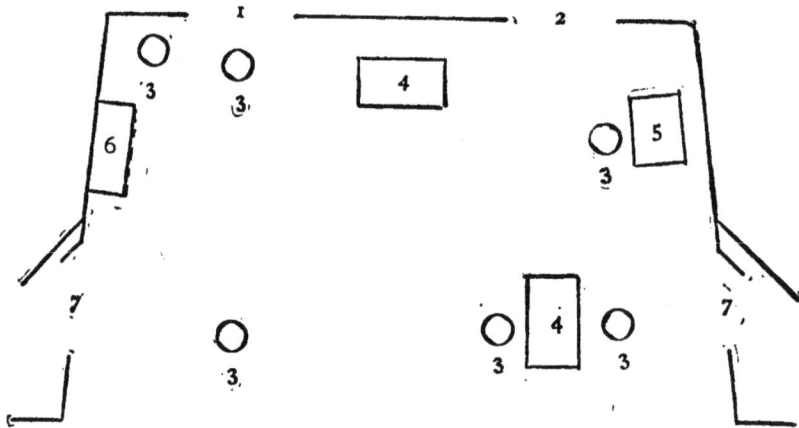

1. Sash window; 2. Opening; 3.* Chairs, with swords on them; 3. Chairs;.
4. Tables; 5. Small writing table; 6. Fireplace or not, as convenient; 7. Doors.
Plain floor.   Lances, boxing gloves, etc., etc., foils and shields hung on sides
and back.   Sporting prints on the scene and photographs.
This scene must have no superfluous furniture.   Cane furniture for choice.

MY "SOLDIER" BOY.

ACT I.

DECEPTION.

" *Oh! what a tangled web we weave*
When once we venture to deceive."

Military Music to open.

SCENE.—MONTAGUE MENDLE'S *house. Half sitting-room; half office. Table* L. C., *on which* MARTHA *is discovered laying breakfast things. Bell ready.*

MARTHA. (*door in flat* L.) Past ten o'clock, and they're not down yet. Rather lucky, as I was late myself; but then I was a-dissipating, as they say, and master and missus wasn't!—not they! They never go nowhere! Sickening I calls it, but there! that comes of making a syrup-suspicious marriage, as missus once told me. He's afraid to let her be seen with him for fear any one should find out about it. Well, that sort of thing wouldn't suit me, and I shall tell Michael so. He's going to propose to me. I felt sure of it last night when he sat next to me at the music hall. Oh! what a beautiful show it was, and there was Michael a-hedging a bit closer to me all the time, and oh! when they turned the lights out for them tabluxes he put his arm around my waist and called me a living picture, I knew as how my fate was sealed. Oh! music halls is fine things. Almost as good as being in a tunnel on a railway. (*a bell heard. Goes to street door; opens it*) Who's that, I wonder? Come in! *Enter* MICHAEL O'DOCHERTY, L. C. *Door in flat* L. C.) What, Mr. O'Docherty? Well, I never!

9

O'D. (*down* R. C.) Go an now! What's the matther wid me front name? I was " Michael " early last avenin', later on " Mike," and " Mik " when we parted. (*kisses her suddenly*)

MARTHA. (L. C.) How dare you?—But what on earth brings you here this morning?

O'D. Shure, it's the greatest good luck in the world. My master sent me.

MARTHA. And who's your master?

O'D. Why, who should he be, but the finest soldier in all the service—Captain Cullendar! I'm afther bringing a letter from him to Mr. Mendle. Here it is. (*produces letter, which he gives to* MARTHA)

MARTHA. (*putting it on table*) All right! he'll see it when he comes down.

O'D. (*coming close to her, embraces her*) Isn't this the blessedest chance?

MARTHA. I was just thinking about you when you came in.

O'D. Were you now? Faith, you couldn't have been thinking about anything betther.

MARTHA. Well, I'm sure!

O'D. And so am I! (*takes her hand*) Do you mind what I said to you last night, when they turned the lights out?

MARTHA. No! I was very angry with you.

O'D. How was I to see you were angry wid me in the dark?

MARTHA. But you—you kissed me!

O'D. I did! and I loiked your cheek. I mean you said, ses you, " I like your cheek!" and I says, says I, " I thought you would," I ses, " I shaved on purpose." Then you said, says you, " Go on!" so I went on. Ah! What a beautiful night altogether.

MARTHA. But, Mike, I've only known you a week.

O'D. A week! me sowl! me brother Tim was married and had a christenin' within a week. (MARTHA *crosses to* L. *of table.* MIKE *crosses to* R. C.) But Tim was a haythen. (*crosses to* R.) Ah! faith it's sad I'll be when we go away from here.

MARTHA. (*following* O'DOCHERTY, *who gets back to* R.) You—you are not going very soon, Mike, are you?

O'D. Me darling, I don't know! (*crosses to* R.) There's

the divil an all to pay wid these riots. We'll stop here as long as they last and longer if they last as long. We are expecting to be called out any day or night for a matther of that.

MARTHA. And suppose you should get killed ?

O'D. An' if I did I'd live forever—in your heart, darlin'. Martha, will you be my widow ? (C.)

MARTHA. I will, I will !

O'D. Faith ! It's meself and half a dozen orphans will be the happiest folks alive. Give us a kiss, my darling. (*he kisses her ; while he is doing so*)

Enter MRS. MENDLE, L. 2 E. *Stands aghast.*

MRS. M. Martha ! (*they separate guiltily*) Who is this ? (MARTHA *crosses at back to* L.)

O'D. (C., *standing at attention*) Private O'Docherty, ma'am, at your service.

MARTHA. If you please, mum, he's come with a note for master from the barracks.

MRS. M. (L. C.) Where is it ?

MARTHA. There, mum ! (*points to table, goes up* L.)

MRS. M. Thank you. (*to* O'D.) Any answer required ?

O'D. I haven't read it, ma'am.

MRS. M. Really ! you need not wait. (*goes* L. *of table*)

O'D. The top of the mornin' to ye, Martha. (*goes up* C.)

MARTHA. (*following, aside to him*) The bottom of the stairs to you—so go at once.

O'D. (*at back*) I'd loike to have had another kiss first.

MARTHA. (*at back*) You've had one already.

O'D. Oh ! That was only a sample. Give me another and I'll order a thousand of them.

MARTHA. Maybe you'll do nothing of the kind—now go ! (*exit door in flat* L. C., O'DOCHERTY)

MRS. M. Martha, I am surprised at you.

MARTHA. (*coming down*) I was a bit surprised myself, mum !

MRS. M. Have you ever seen this person before ?

MARTHA. Oh, yes, mum ! and last night him and me went to the music hall.

MRS. M. He and I.

MARTHA. What, mum—*you* ?

MRS. M. No ! No ! Martha, don't be absurd. I was correcting you.

MARTHA. (R. C.) I didn't think it was wrong, mum, and (*with dignity*) now we're engaged.

MRS. M. Oh, Martha ! what would your master say ? and to a soldier too ! You know how he hates soldiers.

MARTHA. Well, mum, but I'm not obliged to hate what master hates ! I *love* soldiers.

MRS. M. Very well, we won't say any more about it now. Have you called your master ?

MARTHA. Yes, mum !

MRS. M. What did he say ?

MARTHA. He said : " Go to the——

MRS. M. Martha !

MARTHA. What, mum ?

MRS. M. You needn't repeat his language.

MARTHA. It wasn't language, mum. He said : " Go to the post office and fetch me my letters." There they are, mum, on his plate.

MRS. M. Oh ! very well ! Is his breakfast ready ?

MARTHA. Yes, mum ! I'll bring it up now. (*exit* MARTHA, *door in flat* L. C.)

MRS. M. (*sits* L.) Soldiers ! One's life seems to be haunted by soldiers. My husband was intended for a soldier—*I* was a soldier's intended, and now Martha intends to be a soldier—I mean to marry a soldier. The army will lead us into serious trouble one of these days. (*looks at letters on table*) Ah ! Montague seems to have a good deal of correspondence this morning. (*takes up letters and looks them through carelessly, then stops at once*) That writing seems familiar—very familiar ! Oh ! how absurd ! Many men write alike, and yet for the moment I was startled by the similarity. (*throwing it down*) For the moment I was almost frightened. Oh ! what a thing it is to have a secret like mine. I seem to be living in a little deceitful world of my own. Nobody knows I am married to Montague ! Nobody knows I was once engaged to somebody else, and not even my husband knows that *that somebody* else jilted me and that I recovered £2,000 damages against that somebody. I ought to have told him at first, but I put it off and off until I was too frightened.

Re-enter MARTHA *with tray, cup and saucer, cutlet on dish, teapot, plate and milk, etc., and a letter which she gives to* MRS. MENDLE.

MARTHA. Here is a letter addressed to Miss Vaughan —some mistake, mum ?

MRS. M. (*rises, takes it and crosses to* R. C.) No ! quite correct, Martha !—quite right. You ought to re-member nobody knows me as Mrs. Mendle.

MARTHA. But, mum, your letters are generally ad-dressed " Miss Huggins."

MRS. M. Yes, I know. Since I have confided in you so far, Martha—(*aside*) I had better tell her—before I was married I had two maiden names, Huggins— hateful name—was my own ! Vaughan was my step-mother's, which I adopted.

MARTHA. I see, mum !

MRS. M. So for a time at least, Martha, I must rely upon you to be very careful with my letters, or any com-munications you may receive for me.

MARTHA. Certainly, mum, only too glad to do any-thing for you. (*exit door in flat* L.)

MRS. M. (*sits* L. C., *opening letter*) From my lawyer —at last ! (*reads*) " Yourself v. Captain Cullendar. Madam, please sign and return enclosed documents. As you are aware, the amount of £2,000 awarded to you by the court against Captain Cullendar for breach of promise falls due on the 14th of next month, which sum we hope to collect as per your instructions of the 25th March. We are, etc., Copall & Keep." In about a fortnight, then, I shall be relieved of all anxiety ! Montague's mind will be at rest and he none the wiser. I never anticipated the jury would award so much, but, oh ! they were such nice men, and the way my counsel put it. Still I can't help feeling what a scheming little fraud I am—I mean I was. (*puts letter in pocket*)

Enter MONTAGUE MENDLE, R. 1 E. *He has a worried and abstracted air. He is a man of about forty.*

MENDLE. (*crossing to* L.) Morning, Lydia !

MRS. M. Good-morning, darling ! (*rises, crosses to him, kisses him.* MENDLE *crosses back to* R. C.)

MENDLE. My breakfast ready ? (*sits* L. C.)

MRS. M. Quite ready, dear ! (*crosses to* L. I've been

waiting for you.　Now sit down and let me pour you out your tea.　(MENDLE *sits* R. *of table* L.)　You look worried, dear !

MENDLE.　(*mechanically, taking up letters*)　I am worried !

MRS. M.　About——?

MENDLE.　About a dozen times a day on the average.

MRS. M.　What is it particularly at this moment ?

MENDLE.　(*looking round table*)　There is no toast !

MRS. M.　(*smiling*)　I thought it was something serious.　(*rings bell*)

MENDLE.　Lydia, the absence of toast from the breakfast table *is* something serious.　The secret of success in this world is not to make light of so-called trifles.

Enter MARTHA, L. C.

MARTHA.　Did you ring, mum ?

MRS. M.　You have forgotten the toast, Martha.

MENDLE.　Martha, you have forgotten the toast.　(*exit* MARTHA, *door in flat* L.)　You should let me give her the orders, my dear.

MRS. M.　(*sits*)　Monty, you couldn't have slept well.

MENDLE.　Slept !　I have not slept well—since I married you.

MRS. M.　Monty !

MENDLE.　Ah !　you don't know what it is to be the possessor of a hideous secret.

MRS. M.　(*half crying*)　I may be a secret, but I'm not hideous.

MENDLE.　Lydia, I am a huge, living monument of deceit.

MRS. M.　(*aside*)　I am another, only more so.

Re-enter MARTHA *with toast, which she places on table and exits* L.

MENDLE.　This Dam——　(MARTHA *starts*).

MRS. M.　Monty !

MENDLE.　I say this Damocletian sword, which is suspended by a thread above our heads, may descend at any moment.　Oh !　the suspense—the awful suspense.　(*rises suddenly, crosses to* C.)　Lydia, I have half a mind to cut the thread and let it fall.

MRS. M.　What do you mean ?

MENDLE. (*walking off*) This life we are living is not fair to either of us—to you most of all. You are my wife, and yet you are living here in a position that is utterly false.

MRS. M. I am content. (*rises, gets to back of table*)

MENDLE. But you have been seen here—people are beginning to wonder who you are—are beginning to make remarks. Lydia, I shall have to acknowledge—I am convinced that I shall have to acknowledge that you are my wife and—take the consequences ! (*sits* L. C.)

MRS. M. (*in alarm, putting her arms round him*) No ! no ! not that !

MENDLE. Why, what is your objection, Lydia ?

MRS. M. (*in confusion*) Well—your—stepfather— you can't afford it ! You know he would make a beggar of you if he knew you were married. Dearest, we must wait a little longer. (*kneels by him*) He must die one day ! He owes you that at least.

MENDLE. My love, you always look on the bright side of things : but it is my firm impression that he will out-live us both. When he started on his long sea voyage for his health, the doctor said he could not last a week— and—he's lasting still ! I can't go on hiding you for-ever, and I can't keep up the deception about the army forever.

MRS. M. (*rises and crosses to* R.) Oh ! Why did you have a stepfather that was such a—such—a—— (*bell ready*)

MENDLE. Such a fool ! say it, Lydia. I often say it to myself. (*rises*) I assure you I keenly feel the re-sponsibility of being related to such an eccentricity, but we must not forget his immense wealth, and we must not forget the heap of debt I have incurred since our wedding. This deception is wearing me out—I must throw it off.

MRS. M. (*going to him*) But not yet—at any rate, not yet. Wait a little longer, wait at least till—the mid-dle of next month ! Say till the 14th.

MENDLE. Why till the middle of next month ? Why the 14th ?

MRS. M. I'm—I'm superstitious. It is a little fancy of mine dear, that is all. (MENDLE *expostulates with* LYDIA) Don't quarrel with my little fancies. (*tenderly*) You know you were one of them once. (*bell*)

MENDLE. I was *one* of your little fancies. How many have you had, then ?

MRS. M. Now don't be jealous, Monty !

MENDLE. Well, well, let it rest for the present. (*crosses to* L. *of table*) Excuse me while I look at my letters. (*opens letters*) Bills, bills, mostly bills. (*opens another*) What's this ?—from the barracks making a professional appointment. Dear me ! my fame is spreading.

MRS. M. Soldiers again ! (*sighs*)

Enter MARTHA *with card on salver, which she hands to* MENDLE.

MARTHA. Gentleman to see you, sor.

MENDLE. Good heavens ! Take these things away, Martha. (MARTHA *clearing things*—LYDIA *helping*) I've so often said we must have breakfast at half-past seven. Martha, where's my frock coat ?

MARTHA. You've got it on, sor.

MENDLE. I'd no idea it was so late, and the office not uncovered ; go, dear, and fix up my papers in the office, I'll receive him here. Martha, show him in here. (*exit* MARTHA, L. C.)

MRS. M. Well, dear ! good luck with your new client and a heavy bill of costs. (*kisses him on head, and about to exit, turns at door*) But ; above all, remember our secret must be kept just a little longer—till, say, the 14th, to oblige me. (*bell ready, exit door* I E. L.)

MENDLE. (C.) I *do* wonder what Lydia means by the 14th ; but there ! I am sure she has some good reason ! She is a sensible little woman ! Oh ! if I only dared acknowledge her. To have a wife like that and yet be obliged to hide her. To think that if any one happens to see her when they call, I have to introduce her as some one else—my cousin, niece, aunt, anything but what she is. (*crosses to* L., *looks at card*) Captain Cecil Cullendar.

Re-enter MARTHA, *showing in* CAPTAIN CULLENDAR *in mufti, door in flat* L. C.

MARTHA. Captain Cullendar. (*aside* ; CULLENDAR *looks at* MARTHA) He ain't half as handsome as my Mike ! (*exit* L. C.)

CULL. Mr. Mendle ?

MENDLE. (*rises*) That is my name, sir—at your service. (*motions* CULLENDAR *to seat*)

CULL. My name's Cullendar—you have my card—at present stationed with my regiment in this turbulent town. Damn it!

NOTE.—*All these damns are not made emphatic but to be slurred over—pronounced Demmit.*

MENDLE. I beg your pardon.

CULL. Don't mention it; I said damn it; but don't mind me, it's a habit I've got when I'm annoyed, damn it.

MENDLE. Won't you sit down? (MENDLE *sees the toast-rack has been left on the table, tries to put it in the drawer; it won't go in. Runs up with it* C., *puts it on sideboard, comes back to table, finds a slice of toast on table, throws it away up stage.* CULLENDAR *watches him surprised. Offering chair*)

CULL. Ah! thanks! (*sits* L. C.) You're a lawyer, I believe?

MENDLE. (*modestly*) I believe so! (*sits* L.)

CULL. Well, ah! I've come to consult you. I'm in a devil of a mess.

MENDLE. In the nature of——?

CULL. Woman! It always is—woman! Are you a married man?

MENDLE. Yes—I mean—that is—no, no! certainly not!

CULL. Well, make up your mind, damn it.

MENDLE. Are you?

CULL. Worse—I mean I couldn't be in a worse fix if I were. I have an unfortunate and fatal propensity for falling in love, and when I'm in love I propose—and when I propose, they accept—see?

MENDLE. Quite so! And when they accept, you say damn it.

CULL. Just so. Well, I want you to get me out of it.

MENDLE. What do you mean?—out of the habit of swearing?

CULL. Thanks for the hint, damn it. No, out of the consequences. It's easy enough; breach of promise; never had one before, always escaped scot free, but this last one—artful little jade—has been a bit too much for me—sued me! Ah! wants two thousand pounds. Jury gave *me* a lecture, and *her* two thousand pounds.

MENDLE. Well! you paid it?

2

CULL.   No ! I shouldn't have a job for you if I had.
—Can't pay, shan't pay—you get me out of it—see ?

MENDLE.   Easier said than done. When does the
money become due ?

CULL.   Middle of next month—I beiieve the 14th.
(MENDLE *starts*) What's the matter ?

MENDLE.   Nothing, nothing ! (*aside*) I seem to have
heard that date before.

CULL.   Devilish awkward, isn't it ?

MENDLE.   Well, it is rather, but can't you compromise ?

CULL.   I am—don't mention it ; I am always com-
promising—myself—it's hereditary—father just the same,
and bested by a woman Besides, I'm not—ah !—going
to be bullied (*hits the table*).   What's to be done ?

MENDLE.   I really can't say for the moment ; we must
go into details.   What's the lady like—young ?

CULL.   Quite—ladylike and young.

MENDLE.   Pretty ?

CULL.   Devilish !

MENDLE.   That's what influenced the damages.   May
I ask what made you break off the engagement ?

CULL.   My hereditary propensity ! Fell in love with
and proposed to some one else.

MENDLE.   Worse and worse ! And this particular
lady ?

CULL,   Oh, *she* jilted *me !* (*laughs*)

MENDLE.   It doesn't seem to have affected you very
much.

CULL.   No ! rather liked the change—new sensation.
Can't you see your way to help me ?

MENDLE.   My dear sir, you scarcely give one time to
think. Stay ! one moment ; I have an idea.

CULL.   Really.

MENDLE.   Yes ! this girl who has brought the action,
you say she is young and pretty.

CULL.   Both, damn it !

MENDLE.   Well, is there anything against her ?

CULL.   Eh ?

MENDLE.   I mean, against her character.

CULL.   No. Good !—too good !

MENDLE.   Well ! now that Number 2 has thrown you
over, why not take on again with Number 1 ?

CULL.   I don't follow you !

MENDLE. Marry Number 1.

CULL. What ? (*turns to* MENDLE.)

MENDLE. Marry her, and keep the money in the family.

CULL. Well, I'm——

MENDLE. I'm sure you are. If you don't want to part —I mean pay—it is the only way out of your present dilemma ! Would she have you, do you think ?

CULL. Like a bird ! Why, she *loves* me ! (*rises, goes* R. C.)

MENDLE, Then, my dear sir, compromise it. You are certain to marry some one if you go on like this ; why not now ? You might go farther and fare worse. Marriage is always a lottery, but you may draw a prize when you least expect it ; and what is more, by *this* marriage you save a clear two thousand pounds. (*rises, crosses to* C.

CULL. (*coming back*) You're a genius. I've thought of a good many things, but not that. It's a grand idea ! Why not marry ? I'll write to her this very day. Thank you, thank you a thousand times. (*shakes hands*)

MENDLE. Two thousand times—I mean pounds. Don't mention it. I think you will own that my advice was worth following ; it generally is !

CULL. You are a wonderful lawyer.

MENDLE. Thank you. And yet I was not originally intended for the law.

CULL. No ?

MENBLE. My sole surviving relative—my stepfather —destined me for the army. (CULLENDAR *looks him up and down*) It pains me often to think how I have deceived him.

CULL. Deceived him ?

MENDLE. The fact of it is, he was packed off in a sailing ship for a two years' voyage ; so as he quite expected to die, he left enough money behind to enable me to enter the army, but as I didn't like the profession, I turned lawyer.

CULL. Quite so—1 see ; but you don't mean to say you have kept up the deception ?

MENDLE. As he deceived *me* by continuing to live after the doctors had given him up, I was obliged to deceive *him*. He has been abroad for several years, but I have kept him continually informed of my supposed promotion in the service. For you see, each time I'm pro-

moted, he sends me a cheque for two hundred pounds, so
you can imagine I very soon became a colonel. And he
thinks—ha! ha! ha!—excuse me, I can't help laughing,
but he thinks I'm actually the colonel of the 12th Hussars.

CULL. The deuce he does! A colonel! Ha, ha!
My regiment too! Well, *Colonel*, I'm awfully grateful to
you for helping me out of my difficulties, and if ever I
can be of any assistance to you, ah! command me!
Damn it, as my colonel you *do* command me. (*laughs*)

Enter MARTHA, L. C., *with card, which she gives to*
MENDLE.

MAR. (*down* L.) Two ladies to see you, sir.

MENDLE. (*taking card and reading*) Mrs. Morrison
and Miss Morrison. Oh, yes, of course! Show them in
here, Martha! (*exit* MARTHA, L. C.)

CULL. Pardon me! *What* name did I hear?

MENDLE. Morrison—do you know her charming
daughter?

CULL. (*rushes about stage to* R.) You'll excuse my
apparent haste, but have you such a thing as a side door?
Miss Morrison is my Number 2.

MENDLE. What, the lady who jilted you?

CULL. Precisely! Too late, damn it!

Enter MARTHA, L. C., *showing in* MRS. MORRISON *and*
GERALDINE.

MRS. MOR. (*coming forward and shaking hands
warmly*) My dear Mr. Mendle, how are you?

MENDLE. And you? This is quite unexpected.

MRS. MOR. Business! my dear man, business drives.
I'm delighted to see you all the same. You know my
daughter? (*all exchange greetings*)

MENDLE. (L.) Oh, very pleased to see you both.

MRS. MOR. (L. C.) Just come over. (*Sees* CULLENDAR.)
But you're engaged. (*recognizes him*—GERALDINE *also*)
Bless my soul, why, it's Captain Cullendar!

CULL. (R. C., *coming forward*) Ah! delighted to see
you again, Mrs. Morrison. (*rather uncomfortable*) And
ah! you too, Miss Morrison. Won't you shake hands?
(MENDLE *sits* L.)

GERALD. (C.) Oh, yes! (*gives hand, somewhat
coldly, turns her back*)

MRS. MOR. (*aside*) Very unbusinesslike meeting

him again like this. I hope Geraldine won't be foolish and forget her duty. (*goes to* MENDLE, *sits* L. C. *and talks to him*)

CULL. (*to* GERALDINE) Awfully pleased to see you're back again. I mean to see you back again, don't you know. (*they stand back to back. She doesn't answer*) I say I'm awfully pleased.

GERALD. I know you *said* so, but I—I don't know why you should be. I behaved very badly to you.·

CUL. Oh, I don't know.

GERALD. I—I wonder you don't hate me.

CULL. (*aside*) I shall propose if I turn round—I feel it coming on. On the contrary—awfully obliged to you.

GERALD. Are you ? You are not very complimentary.

CULL. Nor were you—when you threw me over.

GERALD. It's not kind of you to mention that.

CULL. I, ah ! beg pardon ; but you see——

GERALD. I don't *want* to see—anything. (*they go up, talking, by the window*)

MENDLE. (*to* MRS. M.) So you know captain Cullendar ?

MRS. MOR. I—er—*used* to know him.

MENDLE. Don't you like him ?

MRS. MOR. I don't know anything against him except he's very unbusinesslike. He once paid his attentions to my daughter—and then circumstances happened to render any engagement out of the question.

MENDLE. Why ?

MRS. MOR. My daughter has to marry someone else—strangely enough, a young man in the same regiment—Lieutenant Allison. That is what has brought me here. His father, one of my oldest friends, died some little time since—left a most businesslike will—and it is about the provisions of this will that I have come here. You see, between ourselves, Mr. Mendle, he is my daughter's future husband.

MENDLE. Really !

MRS. MOR. Positively ! Will drawn to that effect—bound to carry out provision of will. I am sorry though. (*looking round*) that she has met the captain again. He may be dangerous ; just as she was forgetting all about him too.

MENDLE. Well, I think I can relieve your mind a little on that score. Captain Cullendar is going to be married.

MRS. MOR.   You don't say so!. That's splendid, simplifies matters.

MENDLE.   Yes (*rises*). and it is entirely owing to me.

MRS. MOR.   (*rises*) Thank you, thank you! (*shakes hands*) You relieve my mind. (*aside*) I can be friendly with him now.   Oh, Captain Cullendar.

CULL.   (*coming down* R. C.) Mrs. Morrison. (GERALD-INE *comes down to* MRS. MENDLE)

MRS. MOR.   I am delighted to meet you again—delighted! I must admit I was a little—er—surprised at first, owing to our last meeting not being quite—you know—businesslike.   But no matter, let bygones be bygones.   So I hear you are going to be married (*aside*), that strikes a balance.

GERALD.   (*aside*) Married!

CULL.   (*aside* R. C.) Damn it, I'd forgotten all about that. (*looks at* GERALDINE, *aloud*) Married! Ah, yes! I suppose so. (*sighs at* GERALDINE).

MRS. MOR.   Well, I congratulate you, most heartily. (*crosses to* R).

CULL.   Ah, thanks! (*to* GERALDINE) Won't you congratulate me too?

GERALD.   (*with an effort*) I am sure I hope you'll be very happy, (*turns up stage*) Captain Cullendar.

MRS. MOR.   And now I'm going to make use of you. You are the very man I want to see! You have a young gentleman in your regiment named Allison.

CULL.   Old friend of mine.

MRS. MOR.   Good! In barracks now?

CULL.   On duty.

MRS. MOR.   Better!

CULL.   If you care to come round with me I shall be delighted to escort you, and introduce you.

MRS. MOR.   Best! Thank you so much! But you are sure it won't be troubling you?

CULL.   Not in the least. (*aside, crosses to* R.) I shall propose to the mother in a minute, I feel it coming on.

MRS. MOR.   Then we won't lose any more time. Come, Geraldine, my love! (*to* MENDLE) Good-bye, Mr. Mendle, I will come back and seek you later on this business. I shall have a lot of work to put in your way. Marriage settlements and so on. Good-bye! good-bye. (MR. MENDLE *shows them out. Exit in businesslike way*)

GERALD. (*aside*) He is going to be married! Well, there is no escape for me now. (*follows* MRS. MORRISON. MENDLE *comes down* C.)

CULL. (*to* MENDLE) Well, good day Mr. Mendle! and thank you so much for your valuable suggestion. Don't forget if ever I can be of any service to you.

MENDLE. Thank you, I shall remember.

CULL. Command me at any time. (*goes to door* L. C.) *Colonel* Mendle! ha, ha! (*exit door in flat* L. C.)

MENDLE. (C.) Colonel Mendle! it's beastly! how much better Judge Mendle sounds. I've nothing in common with soldiers, I loathe loud colors, and hate a crowd; give me a black gown and blue bag, and a red— I mean white—dirty white wig.

Re-enter LYDIA, I E. L.

MRS. M. All alone, Monty?

MENDLE. Yes, dear; they've gone at last. (LYDIA *crosses to* R. C.) Besides my client, I've had two friends to see me. Mrs. Morrison and her daughter, you've heard me speak of them.

MRS. M. (*puts flowers in vases on mantle*) Oh, yes! I should dearly like to know Miss Morrison.

MENDLE. Well, I will introduce you. (*sits* L. C.)

MRS. M. (R. C.) Don't be absurd! Introduce me— as *whom*?

MENDLE. Oh, of course! I forgot. What a pity I never had a sister. I think I had *better* have one, don't you, Lydia?

MRS. M. (*sits* R. C.) We *might* try that, certainly. Let me see, which of your relations was I last?

MENDLE. The last time, if I remember right, was when young McAndish, the medical student called. He looked so suspiciously at you that I hastily said you were my aunt. He was drinking a whiskey and soda at the time, but I don't think he quite swallowed it.

MRS. M. What, the whiskey and soda?

MENDLE. No, the aunt. His left eyelid closed down slowly over the glass.

MRS. M. And I distinctly heard him murmur something about being a "bit of a one himself." Monty, how many lies a day do you think we tell on an average?

MENDLE. Heaven knows!

MRS. M. Does it? Well, I hope it hasn't kept account of them, or it will be a bad look out for us one day.

MENDLE. (*rises, crosses to* R. C.) It's all my step-father's fault; he should not have imposed such ridiculous conditions upon me. I must be a soldier! I must not get married. I'm sick of all this deceit and subterfuge. If he were here now I'd tell him so to his face. I long to look the whole world in the face and do not care a——

MRS. M. Monty!

MENDLE. A dump.

MRS. M. (*rises*) You must be mad! What will be-come of us: your stepfather—think of him!

MENDLE. Think of him! I've done nothing but think of him for the past twelve months. I don't think a man was ever so much thought of before. And all for what? His filthy lucre! for which I have stooped to deception, masqueraded as a military man, married a wife I dare not acknowledge and piled up a colossal monument of lies. Look at me, Lydia, and say you are ashamed of me.

MRS. M. (*putting her hands on his shoulders*) No! Monty! no! you are my hero! (*aside, takes stage* L.) Oh! what has been his deception compared to mine! (*aloud*) We must face this together, darling, just for a little while longer, this monster and his money.

MENDLE. They can both be——

MRS. M. Monty!

MENDLE. Melted dear, melted.

MRS. M. It might be if he could take it with him, but he *can't*.

MENDLE. Then he can leave it to an asylum for idiots if he likes, then if this suspense goes on much longer I shall benefit by it all the same.

MRS. M. My poor dear!

Enter MARTHA, L. C., *with letter, which she gives to* MENDLE.

MAR. A letter for you, sor. (*exits* L. C.)

MENDLE. (*taking letter and gazing at it intently*) Great heavens, it's from *him!*

MRS. M. No, it can't be!

MENDLE. It is!

MRS. M. (*in a whisper*) Perhaps he's written to say he's dead!

MENDLE. (*in the same tone*) It is. I know his own vile scratchy writing.

MRS. M.   Read it, read it!

MENDLE.   (*opens letter—reads, his face assuming an agonized expression ; then lets fall on the floor and sinks helplessly in a chair* L. C.)   It's all over !

MRS. M.   (*picking it up eagerly and breathlessly*) Then he does write to say he's dead ?

MENDLE.   No ! all over for us, I mean.   Read !

MRS. M.   (*picks up letter and reads, crosses to* R.) " My dear boy, you will be rejoiced to hear that I am quite well and strong again——"

MENDLE.   Skip that, skip that !   Come to the point !

MRP. M.   (*continues reading*)   " Shall be with you to-day early, because it is my last day in the old world." (*crosses to* R. C.)   Then he is going to die to-morrow. What does he mean,—suicide ?

MENDLE.   No ! no ! only going to America—read on !

MRS. M.   (*disappointed*)   Oh !   (*reads*)   " Am going to settle down in New York !   My investments and securities being so shaky, I am compelled to be on the spot. Before I go, however, I yearn to see my soldier boy in full fig at the head of his regiment."   (*looks up*)   Monty !

MENDLE.   (*still collapsed*)   Go on ! go on !   (*rises*)

MRS. M.   (*reading*)   " I want to see him, as I have so often pictured him, surrounded by his comrades in arms. Oh, Monty !   (*throws herself in his arms*)

MENDLE.   (*putting her aside*)   No, he doesn't mean *that* sort of comrade in arms.

MRS. M.   (*continues reading hurriedly*)   " So, as the boat leaves Queenstown to-morrow, shall call on you to-day and invite myself to dine with you at your mess."

MENDLE.   It is a damned mess !

MRS. M.   What shall you do ?   (*crossing down* R.)

MENDLE.   Do !   Why let him come ! and for the first time for years, I'll speak the truth.

MRS. M.   No, anything but that !   It's very hard to tell the truth after all these lies.

MENDLE.   It *must* all come out some day.

MRS. M.   (*aside*)   And all my deception will have been in vain, and I shall lose my £2,000.   Oh, what is to be done ?   (*sits* R. C. ; *aloud*)   It is all my fault, dear ! (*crying*)

MENDLE.   (*goes to her*)   Yours !   Not at all !   *You* didn't make me throw over the army ; you didn't make me a liar—I—mean a lawyer—same thing.   Cheer up,

Lydia ; I declare I feel a positive relief now that we know the worst. (MRS. M *cries on chair*, R.) Don't cry, there's a good girl ; look how jolly I am ! (*sings*) Ha, ha ! why don't you laugh ? It'll be a huge joke to see the old chap's face when he finds out what a fool I've made of him all this time ?

MRS. M. (*very loud—suddenly*) Monty ! (*rises*)

MENDLE. (*starts*) What ?

MRS. M. I've an idea ! We'll carry it through yet.

MENDLE. Carry what through ?

MRS. M. The deception—positively for one day only, as they say in the circus bills—for one day. To-morrow we shall be free !

MENDLE. I don't understand.

MRS. M. He, the monster must never know that you are *not* a soldier.

MENDLE. What are you going to do—dress me up as a toy one—put me on a stand with a gun in my hand and a little cocked hat on my head, or what ?

MRS. M. Don't be absurd ! It's got to be done !

MENDLE. What's got to be done ?

MRS. M. (*backing him to* L. C.) Go to the barracks, make friends with the client you spoke of just now, borrow a uniform, explain your position. It's only for to-day—surely he will oblige you ! Do, do ! for my sake. (*pushes him into chair* L. C.)

MENDLE. Lydia, you're a genius !

MRS. M. I'm a woman ! Go, go ! before he comes.

MENDLE. (*rises suddenly*) I dare say I shall be shot after all. (*going* L.) But I'll do it—I know the very man —he was here just now. He'll help me ! he said so him-self. His last words were : " If ever I can be of any service to you, command me," and I did him a good turn too ; I'll tell you all about that some other time. Lydia, it's a great idea.

MRS. M. Of course it is ! But there is no time to be lost.

MENDLE. I had forgotten though—that is only half the deception ! How about *you !*

MRS. M. Oh ! don't you bother about me. I'll be another relation once again.

MENDLE. That won't wash with him, dear, he knows I haven't got any.

MRS. M. Dear me, that's awkward. Never mind,

I'll be the servant—cook, housemaid, anything. I'll manage it somehow. A few lies more or less won't matter much, as it's for the last time.

MENDLE. Kiss me, my dear ; you are worth your weight in gold.

MRS. M. Not yet, but I soon shall be. (*pushing him off*) Now if you will only be guided by me and do exactly as I tell you, all will come right. Go ! go to the barracks at once.

MENDLE. All right ! I'm off ! (*going up* C., *comes back*) Good-bye ! If the old nuisance comes tell him— what you like.

MRS. M. I'll tell him what he won't like.

MENDLE. I feel the martial spirit filling my breast. " Let me like a soldier fall—on my feet." (*exit door in flat* C. *to* R.)

MRS. M. (*goes to window*) Poor dear Monty, I do hope he will carry it through. He shall not lose a fortune without an effort to save it. A bright uniform, a big bluster, and there you are. (*down* L.) Now, about myself. Well, if he represents a colonel, why not I a General —general servant ? Good ! (*laughs and rings bell on flat* L.)

Enter MARTHA, L. C.

MARTHA. You rang, mum ?

MRS. M. I did. What do you say, Martha, to a holiday ?

MARTHA. I always say—'eaven be praised.

MRS. M. Very well ! I am going to give you one, and while you are away I shall take your place.

MARTHA. Lor, mum ! (*bell ready*)

MRS. M. But you mustn't breathe a syllable to a soul. Have I your promise ?

MARTHA. Mine, mum ? yes, mum ! you see, mum !

MRS. M. I do ! Mum's the word. Now run away, and you needn't be in until quite late to-night. You understand ?

MARTHA. Anything in the world to oblige a good missis, mum !

MRS. M. That's a good girl.

MARTHA. But how about all the cooking ?

MRS. M. I don't suppose I shall do any cooking. (*ring heard*).

MRS. M. Ah! perhaps that is he!

MARTHA. (*runs to window and looks out*) It's an old gentleman, mum.

MRS. M. It must be old Toddenham! Quick, Martha, lend me your cap and apron—I must go and open the door. (*bell*)

MARTHA. Oh, I'll go, mum!

MRS. M. No, no! I must go! you get out of sight; remember I'm the servant now. (*bell*) Quick! (*ring Bus. MARTHA unfastens her cap and apron and MRS. M. hastily puts them on—ring heard again*) Coming! coming! Now you go away, Martha, (*bell*) and don't let me see your face till to-morrow morning. You can go to your sister's. (*bell. Exit door in flat L. C.*)

MARTHA. Thank you! I daresay I *can!* But I daresay I shall do nothing of the sort. Sister's indeed, with all those dear military men about—to say nothing of my Michael! Oh, what a chance! (*looks off at door*) Oh! she's opened the door to him! Well, I never! this is a rum go, and no mistake! I'm off! Sister's indeed! with six children and a paralytic husband! Not me! (*exit door in flat L. 2 E.*)

A few moments' pause and then re-enter MRS. MENDLE, *showing in* JONAS TODDENHAM.

MRS. M. This way, sir, if you please.

TODD. You've kept me waiting a long time.

MRS. M. I'm very sorry, sir, but the basement is so low.

TODD. Basement! Bah! tittivating yourself up, I suppose. Making looks in the isinglass—I mean making eyes in the looking-glass.

MRS. M. (*aside*) He is a funny old gentleman. (*aloud*) Captain Mendle——

TODD. Colonel——

MRS. M. Major.

TODD. Colonel. I'm his stepfather, I ought to know.

MRS. M. Colonel Mendle is at the barracks.

TODD. Barracks! (*with a smack*) Ah! of course! of course! Early morning parade, I suppose.

MRS. M. I beg pardon, sir?

TODD. I wasn't addressing you, young woman. Ah! I ought to have called at the barracks first, barracks, ah! (*as before*)

MRS. M. (*aside*) I'm very glad he didn't.

TODD. (*looking round*) I can't for the life of me see what he wants this house for. Aren't his rooms in the barracks good enough for him. Extravagant young dog. How long has he been living here?

MRS M. Ever since we've been mar—I mean ever since he's been here. (*very hesitatingly*)

TODD. Intelligent class of idiot this. And you're his housekeeper, I suppose?

MRS. M. Well, sir, I do look after him.

TODD. I dare say you do. Come here I want to look after you a bit! I'm rather short-sighted. (MRS. MENDLE *goes to him*) Ah! I thought so. Young! pretty! That's his little game, is it? I daresay you do look after him?

MRS. M. Sir?

TODD. Oh, I know! I know! Young men will be old fools. I'm not such an old fool as not to understand that. And I suppose he makes love to you. Ah, well, perhaps it's not fair to ask that, but look here, young woman, don't you think you're going to entrap him into a marriage, because you're not. I'd cut him off with a shilling.

MRS. M. (*aside*) I am quite sure you would.

TODD. (*sits on a chair* R.) Ah, but he wouldn't do that! Don't look at me like that. He knows which bread his side is buttered. Besides he is a dutiful fellow enough, and most amenable to reason. I only have to express a wish and he carries it out—D-O-N-'T look at me like that. Quite right and proper of course, but it's not all boys who would. You're at it again. But why the devil doesn't he come back? I can't stop here slabbering to a jilly servant girl all day. (*noise of cab ready*)

MRS. M. (*aside*) Silly servant girl! Oh, I should like to shake him! But there, I suppose I must keep my temper. (*aloud*) May I get you a cushion, sir?

TODD. Eh, yes, you may! Why didn't you think of it before. (MRS. MENDLE *gets cushion and puts it behind him*)

MRS. M. (*sweetly*) Is that more comfortable sir?

TODD. It will be when you've done prodding me in the back. Anything would have been more comfortable than that beastly chair as it was.

MRS. M. (*aside*) A cab. It's Monty! He daren't

walk through the streets. Oh, I do hope it's all right. (*rushes to window, fidgetting about*)

TODD. (*testily*) What's the matter? What are you fidgetting about? What's the matter? Can't you stand still, girl?

MRS. M. (*looking off excitedly*) He's got them! He's got them!

TODD. Got 'em! Who's got 'em? I've got 'em? Got 'em? Got what 'em, what? Got 'em—'t 'em got 'ot —ot—ot rot em. (*dies away in a growl*)

MRS. M. How beautiful he looks. (*music, " Let me like a soldier fall." Enter* MENDLE *in full military uniform absurdly fitting. Aside to him*) Oh, you darling! you've managed it then?

MENDLE. Managed it—yes, but these clothes will want as much taking in as he will. (*sees her costume*) Hallo!

TODD. What are you whispering about? eh?

MRS. M. Hush! there he is. (*pointing to* TODD.) He thinks I'm the servant.

MENDLE. (*crossing to* TODD) Ah! my dear steppy, I am delighted to see you.

TODD. My soldier boy! (*they shake hands heartily*)

MENDLE. My dear old dad, welcome home. Let me introduce to you my friend and companion in arms Captain Cullendar. (MRS. M. *turns and sees* CULLENDAR, *shrieks and falls fainting into* MENDLE'S *arms.* MENDLE *hands her over to* CULLENDAR *and rushes to sideboard for brandy*)

CULL. My two thousand pounder!! (*music forte.* MENDLE *returns with brandy,* CULLENDAR *hands her back to* MENDLE *and bolts off door in flat* L. MENDLE *applies brandy decanter to* MRS. MENDLE'S *lips as* TODDENHAM *says*)

TODD. What on earth is the matter with that damned silly servant girl?

Quick Curtain.

END OF ACT I.

ACT II.

"EVICTION."

A few hours between Acts I *and* II.

SCENE.—CAPTAIN CULLENDAR'S *quarters.* L. C. *opening looking on to barrack yard. Doors* R. *and* L. *leading to bedrooms. Music to open.*

O'DOCHERTY *discovered with a drawn sword, and humming an Irish song.*

O'D. (*holding up sword*) How does that look now? Ah, shure, it's just foine, it is! (*sings*)

> " It's as bright as the light
> Of my darlint's own eyes!
> And it kills in the same deadly way."

Faith! they're as bright and as blue as the sky above us (*looks through window*) and that's not blue at all by rayson of a thunder cloud in the front of it : which is like Martha's beautiful eyelids, the blue's behind it all the same. (*whistles*)

Enter ARCHIE ALLISON, L. C. *He looks intensely miserable.*

ALLISON. (*crosses to* R.) Shut up that beastly row. Can't you see I'm worried?

O'D. I can hear you are, sor.

ALLISON. (*crosses to* L.) Has the Captain returned?

O'D. He has not, sor. (*after a pause*) Anything I can do for ye, sor?

ALLISON. (*crosses to* R.) Yes! put a bullet through me. (*during the following dialogue* ALLISON *talks half to himself and half to the audience*)

O'D. Saints above! An' what for?

ALLISON. I've had a legacy left me. A white elephant. (*crosses to* L. C.)

O'D. Holy Moses! Hand him over to the Sergeant Major.

ALLISON. (*sits* L. C., *not noticing*) A white elephant!

A millstone round my neck! A cannon ball round my ankle! A nightmare on my chest!

O'D. Lord save us! Ye're a dead man for the rest of your life.

ALLISON. (*rises crosses to* R., *going across stage and back again*) Why doesn't Cullendar come? I must tell some one or I shall burst. I've had a woman left to me by will, a woman wrapped in a cheque for five and twenty thousand pounds. (*at table* L.)

O'D. That's a comfort, any way.

ALLISON. Is it? Tastes differ——

O'D. May I ask, sor, how it came about?

ALLISON. (*half talking to himself and half to* O'D) I'm not naturally vindictive, but I will. Morrison had kept this sweet thing in cheques to himself!—(*shouts at* O'D.) Why didn't he die intestate?

O'D. Ah! Few of us choose where we'll die, sor. (ALLISON *crosses to* R.) For meself, as long as I live in ould Oireland, I don't care where I die.

ALLISON. (*suddenly*) I won't marry her! (*crosses to* L.) Damned if I will!

O'D. I wouldn't, sor! Damned if I would——

ALLISON. What do you know about it?

O'D. Nothing, sor?

ALLISON: Then shut up!

O'D. I will, sor! (*resumes his work and sings*)

ALLISON. Don't make that infernal noise? I can't stand singing.

O'D. That wasn't singing, sor!

ALLISON. No, my mistake! It wasn't. Well, what-ever it was, chuck it. (*sits* L. C.)

O'D. I'll do that same, sor!

ALLISON. I am irritable to-day! And no wonder.

O'D. No one better right to be, sor!

ALLISON. Don't take any notice of me.

O'D. (*muttering*) I never do, sor!

Enter CULLENDAR, L. C., *looking very downcast.*

CULL. (C.) Hallo, Archie! Morrisons gone?

ALLISON. Yes, but I expect them back by and bye, confound them!

CULL. Hallo! What's up? Don't you like her?

ALLISON. I hate her! She's been left to me in my

father's will like a bit of family plate or a Japanese mug !

CULL. (*warmly*) Don't insult her face.

ALLISON. What's her face to you.

CULL. (*moodily*) Nothing ! Nothing ! I'm booked ! (*crossing to* R. C.)

ALLISON. You look down in the mouth, old chap. Anything wrong ?

CULL. (*thoughtfully, and in a sepulchral voice*) Michael !

O'D. (*down* R.) Sorr ! (*coming forward*)

CULL. Get me a bottle of brandy and a small soda.

O'D. I will, sor ! (*goes to* R. I E.) Faith, he's got a thirst on him. They're as bad as one another, and a trifle worse. (*exit* MIKE, R. I E.)

ALLISON. You look as if you'd had a shock.

CULL. I have ! I've seen a ghost.

ALLISON. Don't jest ! I'm too miserable.

CULL. So am I ! But it's true ; the ghost of an old love.

ALLISON. Which ? Come back to haunt you, I suppose.

CULL. Worse ! To marry me !

Enter MIKE, *with salver, bottle of brandy, syphon of soda and large glass.* CULL. *pours out three parts of a tumbler of brandy,* O'D. *puts in about a tablespoonful of soda,* CULL. *shouts, " That'll do."*

ALLISON. That's bad.

CULL. It's too true. I must marry her unless I want to part with £2,000. (MIKE *puts tray on table,* L. C., *then goes up* C. ; *polishes sword*)

ALLISON. My case precisely, only the amounts differ. But I've never heard anything about her. Who is she ?— what is she ?—where is she ?

CULL. (*sits* R. C.) It—I mean she—wasn't worth mentioning. She was only one of many I had promised to marry ; but she means that I must stick to my promise or take the consequences.

ALLISON. What's her social position ?

CULL. She hasn't got one. When I first knew her she was a governess, but she has descended since then, and now picture it ! Think of it ! She is a sort of general servant to Mendle, the lawyer.

3

O'D. (*who has been listening at back, drops sword with a loud crash*) Blazes! (*shakes his fist at* CUL-LENDAR, *and then stands attention.* CULL. *wheels round, back to audience*)

CULL. (*rises*) What's the matter? Clumsy idiot! Get out!

O'D. Yes sorr. (*aside as he goes,* L. C.) Martha, Martha! You're as bad as the rest of 'em. I'll niver thrust woman again, nor man neither, for a matter of that. (*exit* L. C.)

CULL. I shall have to get another man.

ALLISON. (L. *of table*) Oh, they're all alike. My man's just as bad. I say, Cecil, about these girls; we are both in the same boat it seems. (*sits* L.)

CULL. (*sits* R. *of table*) I don't care if you pull the plug out and scuttle us.

ALLISON. Nor do I! (*after a pause*) Is there no escape?

CULL. Not for me—but you are all right.

ALLISON. I'm all wrong! I've got to marry Miss Morrison or forfeit a fortune.

CULL. Well, why not marry her? She's a very nice girl. I think you're a very lucky chap.

ALLISON. How is it you know her?

CULL. I was engaged to her once.

ALLISON. The deuce you were!

CULL. Oh, it's nothing.

ALLISON. (L. *on table*) Is there any girl you were not engaged to once?

CULL. (*sits on edge of table* L. C.) Very few decent looking ones. I can't help it. When I meet a pretty girl I don't mean to propose, but I do; it breaks out like measles. It's my nature to be complimentary to women, and once you start a train of conversation on the broad rails of compliment, it goes on and on, gathering steam, flying past the wayside stations of coquetry, flirtation, amusement and platonic friendship, till it runs at last into the siding of " engagement " or meets with an accident and crashes along down the embankment of matrimony, or in trying to pull up you find yourself landed at the busy junction Breach of Promise. (*crosses to* R.)

ALLISON. (C.) Ah, you should have lived in the days of stage coaches. You'd have had more leisure to observe the danger.

CULL. (*gloomily*) I don't know. It was slower in those days, certainly, but you got there just the same.

Re-enter O'DOCHERTY *with a letter.*

O'D. Letther for you, sor! (CULL. *takes it.* MIKE *turns up* C.)

CULL. (*takes letter, opens it and reads*) " Forgive me for that scene this morning. Our meeting startled me. I went off so suddenly that I had not time to speak to you. I must see you at once. Please send a line by bearer, to say you won't refuse me this request. Lydia." It's from her. She wants to see me. I thought she would. (*crosses to writing-table* L.) Ah, well, I suppose I must consent. Wait a minute. (ALLISON *crosses to* R.)

O'D. I will, sor !

CULL. (*goes to desk, takes note-paper and writes*) " Come when you like, shall be in all day. Cecil." Who is waiting ?

O'D. A boy, sor, *this* time.

CULL. Give him that note. (*rises, gives note to* O'D.)

O'D. Yes, sor. And, if you please, there are TWO MORE ladies waiting down below.

ALLISON. The Morrisons ! Oh, lor !

CULL. Then show them up, quick. (*exit* O'DOCHERTY L. C.)

ALLISON. (R.) You see, there's no escape for me, so let us put off the evil day as long as possible.

Enter MRS. MORRISON *and* GERALDINE L. C.

MRS. MOR. (R. C.) Well ! We've been rather longer than we intended, but these people are so slow, so un-businesslike. Had a bit of lunch at the Shelton, did a bit of shopping—everything much too dear—and we shall soon be ready for a cup of tea. (*sits* R. C.)

ALLISON. Tea ! Pity tannin isn't deadly poison.

CULL. (*To* GERALDINE *up* C.) You have arrived at rather an unfortunate time. The country is in a terrible state, we are held in readiness to be called out daily, and, to add to our difficulties, our colonel is laid low with fever ; still we await the arrival of a new command to-night.

ALLISON. Are you going to make a long stay ?

MRS. MOR. Well—that depends ! Must give you two young people a chance of making each other's aquaintance, you know. (*aside to* ALLISON) I'm sure you'll get along very comfortably with the dear girl.

ALLISON. Very dear !

MRS. MOR. Eh ?

ALLISON. I said very—dear—girl.

MRS. MOR. You don't seem enthusiastic.

ALLISON. I am not of an enthusiastic nature. (*aside*) I'll make her daughter hate me.

MRS. MOR. Your poor father was so anxious about this marriage. Geraldine was his constant companion during his last illness, and I remember his last words were—dear me, Geraldine ! what were poor Mr. Allison's last words ?

GERALD. (*who has been talking to* CULLENDAR *at back*) Isn't it an awful bore ?

MRS. MOR. Eh ? No, no ! What are you talking about, child ?

GERALD. Pardon me—what did you say ?

MRS. MOR. (*rises*) I was telling Mr. Allison how kind and attentive you were to his father during his last illness. He—he would like to thank you himself. (*passes* GERALDINE *over to* ALLISON, *talks to* CULLENDAR, *goes up* C.)

GERALD. (R. C., *to* ALLISON) Please don't, Mr. Allison ! It was nothing.

ALLISON. (R. *absently*) Eh ! Wasn't it ? (*aside*) It has led to most awful consequences.

GERALD. (*suddenly*) Mr. Allison !

ALLISON. What ?

GERALD. Can't you take a violent dislike to me ?

ALLISON. I have ! I mean——

GERALD. Oh ! Don't apologize ! I—I—I simply hate you !

ALLISON. (*shaking her hand*) Thank you ! thank you ! exceedingly—excessively.

GERALD. But we've got to be married !

ALLISON. *Got* to be married ! It's quite enough to make two people hate each other. Besides, there might be a funeral first !

GERALD. Ah ! that's one easy way out of it !

ALLISON. Bravo ! Then you're determined to kick over the traces, eh ?

GERALD. Quite ! And, if necessary, splinter the parental splash board, too.

ALLISON. Your Ma will be awfully wild !

GERALD. I don't care! Anything is better than being chained to a log for life.

ALLISON. Thank you, we're getting on splendidly! (*they turn up to window* C. *He shakes her hands effusively as he leads her up back*)

MRS. MOR. (*coming down* C.) No, no! I shall fix up the wedding as soon as possible. (*comes down with* CULL.) I hate unnecessary delay. It isn't businesslike. Once a thing is settled, carry it out. Know first what you are going to do, then do it, that's my motto.

CULL. (L. C.) I suppose both parties agree to the sacrifice?

MRS. MOR. Sacrifice?

CULL. I mean—well—er—after all, you know, it is a sacrifice, offered up at the altar.

MRS. MOR. Ha, ha! Quite so! But it will not be much of a sacrifice in this instance; they'll gain a fortune by it. Why, they must be in the seventh heaven of delight.

CULL. (L. C. *glancing at them*) They look it. (*to* MRS. MOR.) Yes! I suppose money is of more consequence than love. (ALLISON *and* GERALDINE *are standing back to back*)

MRS. MOR. Love! Bosh! No one marries for love! No business woman, I'll answer for it.

CULL. I don't know (*aside*). It's coming on. (*aloud*) I've heard of it being done.

MRS. MOR. Only by fools, and they'll do anything.

CULL. It's gone off.

Enter O'DOCHERTY, L. C.

O'D. (*to* CULL.) Lady to see you, sor! (*aside*) Another!

CULL. One moment. (*aside*) Can't have a scene before these people.

MRS. MOR. Business, eh? Good! We had better leave you.

CULL. (*eagerly*) Thank you! Probably you'd like to have a look round. Allison will look after you, won't you? (*aside to* ALLISON) Trot 'em round the barrack yard half a dozen times.

ALLISON. (*aside*) You're a nice sort of friend, you are. (*to* MRS. MOR.) Much pleasure—this way. (*hurries them out; exeunt* ALLISON, MRS. MOR. *and* GERALD, L. C.)

CULL. (*crossing to* R.) She has come then! I knew she would. She will be rather staggered when she hears I mean to marry her after all. (*to* O'D.) Show the lady in.

O'D. I will. (*aside ; going to door*, L. C.) Another of 'em, and still he isn't satisfied, the haythen Turk. (*going*) Oh, Martha, Martha !

CULL. (*alone*) It's doocid unpleasant to be forced to eat your own words, unswear your own oaths, and make love all over again; it's like warming up cold hash. (*crosses to* L. *Enter* MRS. MENDLE, *veiled, shown in by* MIKE. MIKE *exits* L. I E.) Well, and how do you do? I didn't have time to say it this morning.

MRS. M. (R. C.) I was very foolish! The sudden meeting upset me.

CULL. So it did me! I never thought to see you like that.

MRS. M. Like what?

CULL. (L. C.) Why, like a dashed servant, you know.

MRS. M. No, I suppose not! (*sighs*) It's a great come-down. (*sits* R. C.) Fancy you're knowing my—my master !

CULL. I called on him to-day to consult him about you.

MRS. M. About me?

CULL. Yes ; I wanted to know if he could help me out of this fix.

MRS. M. Well, and what did he advise?

CULL. He said, ah ! the only way to avoid paying the money was to—ah !——

MRS. M. Yes? Yes?

CULL. (*rises*) To marry you !

MRS. M. To what? He couldn't have told you that.

CULL. He did, on my honor.

MRS. M. But the thing's impossible. I'm—I mean he —that is, Mr. Mendle, doesn't know the circumstances, (*takes step* R.)

CULL. I told him all about it.

MRS. M. Not who I was?

CULL. Of course I did ? Why not?

MRS. M. Why not! Don't you see? If he knew that I was me, I mean I was he—he—we ; he would—he would send me away. Please, please don't tell him !

CULL. Of course I didn't tell him who his own servant was.

MRS. M. Oh!—I see—thank you, thank you. I am sure you would be generous. (*aside*) Nice mix up. (*sits* R. C.)

CULL. (*coming down* R. C.) But what on earth has made you come down to this?

MRS. M. To what?

CULL. To being a domestic servant. I am devilish sorry! I am, upon my soul. (*aside*) She's looking provokingly pretty.

MRS. M. There was nothing else left for me to do, when you—jilted me.

CULL. I begin to think I behaved like a brute.

MRS. M. The jury said so!

CULL. (*sits*) Lydia—you—you must promise not to press me for these damages—I've paid costs.

MRS. M. But what am I to do? The matter is out of my hands.

CULL. It's no use, you mustn't pursue it—it will ruin me.

MRS. M. Well, I——

CULL. I know what you are going to say.

MRS. M. (*aside*) It's more than I do.

CULL. (*up and down stage*) You are going to tell me that it's only tit for tat; that socially I have ruined your prospects. That instead of fulfilling my promise and giving you some position in the world as my wife, I basely left you to earn a precarious livelihood as a domestic servant. Go on; I deserve it. (*crosses to* L.)

MRS. M. (*rises, crosses to* C.(I assure you——

CULL. But thank Heaven it is not too late to make reparation. Lydia, I have been thinking it all over, and I have decided to take the solicitor's advice, and marry you!

MRS. M. But you can't—I can't—that is *you* couldn'—I mean—oh! don't you understand! It can't be—it's impossible!

CULL. Ah! You are thinking of the difference in our positions. That is generous of you, but you are a lady, and I mean to act honorably.

MRS. M. Thank you! Thank you! (*they shake hands. Aside*) It's like flirting with bigamy.

CULL. (*aside*) She doesn't seem so very pleased; perhaps, after all, she would have preferred the money. Women are so mercenary. (*aloud, crosses to her, puts his arm around her waist*) Well, Lydia, what do you say ?

MRS. M. (*pushes him away*) I can't say anything just now. I—I must think it over ; but please, please don't mention the matter again to my—I mean to my master.

CULL. You seem to have a great fear of your employer.

MRS. M. I have. I wouldn't have him know about this for the world.

CULL. Does he treat you badly then ?

MRS. M. Oh, no ! He's the dearest—I should say, the kindest master in the world, but he is so jealous. (*goes* R.)

CULL. Jealous ? You don't mean to say he makes love to you himself ? (*following her* R.)

MRS. M. (*aside*) Each step I'm sinking deeper. (*hesitating*) He—has done !

CULL. The monster ! I'll kill him ! (*going* L.)

MRS. M. (*crosses to him*) No, no !

CULL. How pretty she is. (*aside*) 'Pon my honor, I never appreciated her before. (MENDLE'S *voice heard outside*)

MENDLE. This way, Steppy. Don't shake hands with the sentry.

MRS. M. Great Heavens ! he's here. Where can I go ? He mustn't see me ! Hide me ! Hide me somewhere.

CULL. What does it matter ? I've proposed, I am accepted again. I'll introduce you.

MRS. M. No, no ! For Heaven's sake no ! He'd kill me.

CULL. Kill you ?

MRS. M. I mean you.

CULL. That's quite another matter. Well ! there's only my room, but as you're to be my wife, there's no harm. In here. (*goes* R. *and opens door for her. Exit* MRS. M. *into room,* R. I E.)

CULL. She's prettier than ever ! Poor persecuted girl. (MENDLE'S *voice heard again*)

MENDLE. (*stands in front of window* C. *outside*) We can get a snack in the canteen.

CULL. Ah ! there he is ! He's brought back the Colonel's uniform, I suppose ! it was a risky thing to do, lending him old Roscoe's uniform ; but he's in bed and can't move. (*goes and looks off*) Why, he's got them on still! All on! (*crosses to* L.)

Enter MENDLE, *followed by* TODDENHAM, L. C.

MENDLE. Make yourself at home, Steppy. (TODDEN-HAM *always places his hat on small table in centre of flat at back*)

MENDLE. (C., *aside to* CULL.) He would come! Keep it up! Keep it up! It's only for to-day. Scratch my back hard, and I'll scratch yours.

CULL. (L. C., *to* MENDLE) I'll do my best, but it's an awful risk.

MENDLE. Yes, all ours. That's the Peninsular. (*pointing to shields*) That's Waterloo. (*points to other shield*) We shot all those. (*points to lances and gloves*, L. C., *on wall back*)

TODD. (R. C. *to* CULL.) I hope you don't mind, Captain Cullendar. I asked Colonel Mendle to bring me here.

CULL. Oh! not at all! Delighted to see any friend of the Colonel's.

TODD. I am so fond of the army—anything military! You see I made my fortune by buttoning up the army. I myself have often been mistaken for an officer and a gentleman, and nothing could give me greater happiness than to witness my boy's present proud position. To be Colonel of his regiment too, in so short a time!

CULL. Yes, his promotion was rapid—very rapid! Almost unprecedented, I should say.

TODD. Wonderful! wonderful! (*to* MENDLE) But I have still one regret.

MENDLE. And that is?

TODD. That you have never been shot at.

MENDLE. Eh?

TODD. I mean never taken part in some battle. I don't know whether I shouldn't like you better with a cork eye or a glass leg. There's a lot of romance to me in having an arm shot off. Look at Nelson! Still there's time enough for that, thank goodness. (*shakes hands*)

MENDLE. Thank you! Thank you!

TODD. Now! tell me something about your duties. Can't you tip us word of command, or fire something off, or wave a flag.

MENDLE. (*aside to* CULL.) What the devil do I do?

CULL. (*aside*) Bully the men principally.

MENDLE. (C.) Ah! You mustn't think that a soldier's life even in barracks is all—is all—thingumbob. (CULLENDAR *pushes* MENDLE) I assure you, there are times when one feels the responsibility of one's—what you may call it. (CULLENDAR *pushes* MENDLE, *who falls against* TODDENHAM) Only yesterday, in the small hours of the morning, when I was doing Sentry-go!

TODD. (R.) What?

CULL. (L. *aside to him*) Idiot! Remember, you are a Colonel!

MENDLE. I'd forgotten that! I mean when I had to say to a Sentry "Go!" I dismissed him for insubordination. He was very rude—he didn't go, so I had to go for him, and I went for him, and found him drunk.

TODD. How terrible! (CULLENDAR *sits* L. C.)

MENDLE. Oh! Very sad, wasn't it?

TODD. Well?

MENDLE. Well, the sad part has to come.

TODD. Sad part to come, eh! Wait a minute,—I always like to be comfortable when there's anything sad—(*takes chair*) Well? Now then!

MENDLE. Well! he burst into tears, and said he had a mother.

TODD. Alive?

MENDLE. Oh, quite.

TODD. How sad!

MENDLE. And that day she had taken him to (*makes circular movement with his arm as though fishing for an excuse*)

TODD. The great wheel?

MENDLE. No, to the wax-works.

TODD. What for?

MENDLE. (*aside*) Damned if I know (*turns to* CULLENDAR) what for?

TODD. Eh?

MENDLE. What for? Oh! To rouse his martial spirit.

TODD. And did it?

MENDLE. (*aside*) Hang it, he wants to know such a lot. (*aloud*) Oh yes, so much that he fainted at the sight of Wellington, and his mother had to take him to the refreshment room—and that accounted for his disgraceful state, my lud! (MENDLE *unconsciously drops into the law jargon*)

CULL. (*laughs. Aside*) He is the best liar I ever met; no wonder he wanted to be a solicitor.

TODD. Wonderful! wonderful! And what became of him?

MENDLE. Forty shillings or a month. His mother paid it.

CULL. (*rises*) No, no! You sent him to the cells.

MENDLE. Well, I can, it isn't too late. (*to* TODD.) We sent him to the cells! You haven't seen the cells? (*aside to* CULL.) Take him and show him the cells, and lock him up by mistake. Come and see the cells.

TODD. I will. I wouldn't miss a good *cell* for anything, but first I want to know what became of him when he came out.

MENDLE. (*aside*) Oh, dash it all, I can't keep on. (*aloud*) When he came out, it preyed on his mind, so he took to drink and died—and I had to compensate his widow—I mean wife—that is, mother—and bury him.

TODD. And did you bury him?

MENDLE. Oh, yes, buried the lot.

TODD. And you paid it all?

MENDLE. Every penny.

TODD. It must have cost you a pretty penny?

MENDLE. Oh, six-and-eight-pence. I mean I paid every penny.

TODD. My poor boy, you must allow me to make it up to you. (*takes out pocket-book with notes*)

MENDLE. Oh, no! on no account!

TODD. I insist! I insist! Will a hundred square the wax-work mother? After all, it was to please me that you entered the army, and I cannot allow you to suffer in pocket for doing your duty. (*gives notes and goes up* R.)

MENDLE. (*aside*) Lying pays even better than I thought it did.

CULL. (*aside*) I say, I ought to stand in.

MENDLE. You shall, my boy—so you shall. (MENDLE *tries to put notes in his pocket but can't find pocket*) I say, where's the pocket?

CULL. Never mind, give them to me. (MENDLE *puts notes in his hat, goes up to window and calls "Lights Out!"*)

TODD. (*to* CULL.) You must be very proud of your Colonel, sir !

CULL. Oh, I am ! (*aside*) If only for his masterly lying.

Enter O'DOCHERTY, L. 1 E.

O'D. You're wanted, sor !

CULL. By whom ?

O'D. The Colonel, sor !

TODD. What Colonel ?

CULL. Colonel Roscoe ; oh, we've several colonels. (*aside*) I'm at it now.

MENDLE. Yes, we have lots of colonels. First-class regiment.

TODD. Oh, I didn't know. (*goes up back*)

CULL. (*anxiously*) But—er—he's still in bed, eh ?

O'D. Yes, sor ! But he wants to get up !

CULL. He mustn't ! It would be his death. (*aside*) Besides, he might miss his uniform.

O'D. By your lave, sor, the Colonel seems a bit strange in his mind. He insists on a full dress parade.

CULL. Great Heavens ! he's raving, he must not get up to-day ; he is too ill. The doctor distinctly said yesterday that it would be highly dangerous.

O'D. Yes, sor ! (*looking at* MENDLE) If he were to get up it would be highly dangerous for somebody !

CULL. With the fever still on him, it would be madness. I must go to him at once. Excuse me for five minutes.

MENDLE. (*aside to* CULL.) Keep him in bed, drug him, sit on his head.

CULL. (*aside to* MENDLE) You don't know Roscoe. If he's made up his mind one way a locomotive could not move him another. (*exit* L. 1 E.)

MENDLE. (*taking* O'D.'s *hand*) Do what you can. (*turns* R.)

O'D. (*going*) Well, I see all, and I hould me whist. (*exit* L. 1 E.)

TODD. Well, my boy, I shall remember this day as long as I live.

MENDLE. (*aside*) So shall I.

TODD. But you mustn't forget I am going away to-morrow. (*with emotion*) I may never see you again.

MENDLE. I'm very glad.

TODD. What?

MENDLE. (*correcting himself*) I'm very glad you were able to spend at least this one day with me.

TODD. I'm sure you are, my boy. Oh! there's one thing I quite forgot to mention; I don't like that servant girl of yours.

MENDLE. What, Martha?

TODD. I don't know what her confounded name is, but you must get rid of her. She is too pretty for a single man to have about the house.

MENDLE. Well, it never struck me that she was pretty.

TODD. Didn't it? it did me. You should have seen the way she looked at me. However, that's neither here nor there. Well, now, I've got an idea. As you know, I'm going to America to-morrow, and there are no servants there to speak of, and I shall want some one to look after me, and be my housekeeper, and so on, so I've determined to take her with me.

MENDLE. (*aside*) Heavens! He means Lydia!

TODD. She's an artful hussy; I can see it in her eyes, and she'll be getting round you; probably entrapping you into marriage.

MENDLE. But I assure you——

TODD. Well, anyhow, if she comes with me you will have no temptation, so we will consider that settled. I like someone young about me, and I am too old to be tempted.

MENDLE. You can take her by all means, if she will go.

TODD. Go? Of course she will. I'll make it worth her while. But come, my boy, it's getting dark outside and I haven't seen any of the sights yet, not even the cells. (*takes hat and goes to door* R.)

MENDLE. (*aside*) Where *has* Cullendar gone? I know I shall be detected by some of those beastly soldiers. I dread to think of the consequences. (*not observing* TODD.)

TODD. (*at door*) I suppose we can get out this way. (*goes and opens door* R., *sees* MRS. M., *bangs door and turns to* MENDLE) Montague, you are deceiving me.

MENDLE. I—I? What's the matter?

TODD. (*severely*) There *is* something between you and that young woman.

MENDLE. What young woman?

TODD. That pretty servant of yours. I suspected it all along. I didn't think, though, she would have the audacity to follow you here.

MENDLE. (*in an agony of suspense*) Follow me here! what do you mean ?

TODD. She is in that room now !

MENDLE. Room ? Lyd—Martha ! Impossible !

TODD. I tell you she's there. (*opens door again and calls*) Young woman, come out ; come out, I say ! No nonsense with me. (*turns to* MENDLE *reproachfully*) And in *your* room, too.

MRS. MENDLE *enters slowly ; comes to* C.

MENDLE. (*staggering back aghast*) Lydia here ! And in *his* room.

MRS. M. (C. *Aside to* MENDLE) Keep quiet, I will explain by and bye. (*crosses to* R.)

MENDLE. (L. *Feebly*) Explain ? I—I—(*aside*) in *his* room, too.

TODD. (C. *To* MENDLE) Don't say anything ; leave her to me ! (*to* MRS. M.) Young woman, your un-blushing effrontery has inexpressibly shocked me. Whether or not your master was a party to this decep-tion I am not prepared to say, though judging by his guilty appearance I should imagine he was. If so, his conduct is unworthy his rank as an officer and a gentle-man, and I warn him that I will cut him off with a shill-ing, unless he instantly severs his infamous intrigue with you. Now, don't answer me, but listen. I am going to America to-morrow, and in order to remove temptation from his path, I shall take you with me. Not a word ! my mind's made up ! (MENDLE *crosses to* MRS. M. *To* MENDLE) Come ! Takes Mendle's arm and drags him up stage. Not a word. Come. (*exit* TODD., *half drag-ging* MENDLE, *who attempts to speak to* LYDIA)

MRS. M. 'Pon my word, I think I had *better* go to America with him ; it is the only way out of this dilem-ma. (*bell off* L. I E.) Montague will never believe me again. How can I ever explain my presence here ? I am a most unhappy woman, and I was doing it all for the best. Oh ! you wretched old man, how I hate you ! it is all your fault. (*half crying*) Why are wretched old men always so rech—I mean rich. (*bell. Voice heard off* L. I E.) Someone coming. (*bolts back into room* R. I E.)

Enter COLONEL ROSCOE. *He is dressed in pyjamas under white dressing gown, as though just out of bed. He has an absent, wandering manner.*

NOTE.—*Bell rung off in* ROSCOE'S *room, first time at* " *out of this dilemma*." *Second time at* " *always so rich*."

ROSCOE. (*crosses to* L. C.) I'll not be neglected in this manner! I, the colonel of this regiment! Anything any minute may happen to me in my state. Where the devil is everybody? I can't make my man hear. Everything is locked up, and I can't find my keys. There's some confounded game on! I'll—I'll court-martial the lot if—if (*catches hold of table*) Hallo! hallo! I feel very shaky still; the doctor said yesterday I'd been delirious—had a touch of brain fever. I only wonder I wasn't killed outright, being thrown off that brute of a horse. I mustn't ride him again; I'll sell him to a friend! (*staggers slightly*) Hallo! this won't do! (*sits* L. C.) I'm weaker than I thought. I had better go back to bed again. (*sees brandy on table* L. C.) Ah! brandy! It's against orders, but a drop of this will do me good! (*pours out brandy and drinks*) That's better! I shall be all right directly. My head feels strangely light though. I hope I'm not going to have a relapse. (*sits in chair and sips brandy*)

Enter TODDENHAM—*glow of setting sun on back cloth.*

TODD. I must have another talk with that servant girl, and settle this American affair; she is pretty. (*looks round*) Not here; where's she gone, I wonder? (*sees* ROSCOE) Hallo! who's this?

ROSCOE. A stranger! what does he want here? (*aloud*) Well, sir!

TODD. (*aside*) Strange looking party; comic uniform, or has he been having a bath? (*aloud*) Pardon me, sir, but mind you don't catch cold! (ROSCOE *drinks*) That's right, have a drop of spirit!

ROSCOE. Don't dictate to me, sir! Who are you?

TODD. (*aside*) What a violent man. (*aloud*) Please, don't get excited.

ROSCOE. Excited! sir, do you know who you are talking to?

TODD No! and I don't want to. But whoever you

are, you are a very foolish old gentleman to walk about like that! You look very ill! Go and dress yourself. (*check lights slightly* INSIDE *room.* OUTSIDE *in the barrack yard the lights gradually change from yellow to red and then gradually die out altogether till quite pitch dark.*)

ROSCOE. (*almost speechless with indignation*) Well —I'm—what is your business in the barracks, and who is responsible for your introduction? Answer me—answer me?

TODD. Certainly, if you only keep cool! I am a guest of the Colonel's.

ROSCOE. (*sinking back in his chair and gasping*) The—the Colonel's!

TODD. To be sure! I'm his stepfather.

ROSCOE. (*aside*) That brandy has got into my head —or else I'm going mad. (*to* TODD.) Say it again!

TODD. You must be very deaf! (*goes to him and shouts in his* R. *ear*) I distinctly said that my boy is the Colonel! (*changes to* ROSCOE'S L. *ear*) Perhaps the other ear is larger. I said my boy is the Colonel of this regiment, and I am here at his invitation.

ROSCOE. But what Colonel? Which Colonel, whose Colonel?

TODD. Oh, dear! you must be very ill, not to know your own Colonel! (*gets to* L. *of table*)

ROSCOE. Do you want to drive me mad? *I'm* the Colonel of this regiment.

TODD. My dear sir, you really are very ill, for now you're rambling. Take my advice, drop that brandy and try soda water. Would you object to my feeling your pulse?

ROSCOE. (*getting round to* L. TODD. *crosses to* C.) I'd feel your head with the poker, if I could only get at it. I don't know, though, there's something wrong. Am I going mad, or is this a result of the fever? I certainly feel very strange—I think I'll go back to bed and wait till somebody comes and tells me who I am. I don't feel quite sure. (*to* TODD.) I suppose you are quite *sure* I'm not the Colonel? (*lights* INSIDE *down to half*)

TODD. I'm morally certain of it. But there, there! If you don't get excited, and live and get your hair cut you may be one of these days. If my boy were here he'd tell you the same thing.

ROSCOE. Who the devil is your boy ?

TODD. I keep on telling you the Colonel of this regiment.

ROSCOE. Oh! then I'm your boy—I'm much worse than I thought I was. I say, suppose you were ill——

TODD. Yes, I have been ill several times.

ROSCOE. And thought yourself worse than you were, and then thought you couldn't be worse than you were because you weren't yourself, but someone's boy, who was worse than your—who—oh !—I give it up !

TODD. I gave it up at once.

ROSCOE. Take me back to bed.

TODD. Take my advice and see a specialist.

Enter CULLENDAR, L. C. *Lights gradually go down on the stage. It is quite dark in the barrack square.*

CULL. (C. *aside*) Hallo, they're together !

TODD. (R. C.) I say, Captain Cullendar, there's a poor drivelling lunatic at large in a bath towel without buttons, I should put him in irons.

ROSCOE. (L. C., *in a helpless sort of a way*) I say, Cullendar, you are Cullendar, aren't you ? Just tell me who I am. I'm quite uncertain.

CULL. You shouldn't have got up, sir ! you *know* you shouldn't ! you're not yourself at all.

ROSCOE. That's what *he's* been telling me ! (*crossing to* TODD.) You see you were quite right. (*shakes hands*) Oh, my poor head ! I apologize, Mr. Whats-your-name. (*warning for lights to go up*)

CULL. Let me help you back to your room, sir. You'll be all right in a day or two, if you keep quiet.

ROSCOE. But I wish I knew who I was ! I should feel more settled.

CULL. Now don't worry about it, or you'll be worse. Come back to bed, and we'll send and inquire at the war office.

TODD. Yes ! take him back to bed ; and label him, and don't let him go wandering about like that any more. (*aside*) *I* should put him in a straight waistcoat.

ROSCOE. (*at door*) Take me away, Cullendar ! and meanwhile try and find out who I really am.

CULL. You'll be all right in a day or two. Come along !

ROSCOE. And drive that away ! (*pointing to* TODD)

4

It worries me, it worries me ! (*repeats off ; exeunt* Ros-COE *and* CULL. R. I E.)

Enter MIKE, *who lights the two gas brackets with taper in a socket.*

TODD. I wonder who he is ! He's very strange in his manner, and what an extraordinary delusion to fancy he is the Colonel ! Poor gentleman, his mind is evidently affected ! Montague must be told about him. I had better go and find him. (*sees* MIKE) Have you seen Colonel Mendle ? (*turns, sees, lighted taper, knocks it out with his hat*) Do be careful, you'll be letting guns off.

MIKE. He's in the canteen, sir.

TODD. I must find him at once, come along. (*exit, followed by* MIKE)

Re-enter CULLENDAR, L. I E.

CULL. What an unfortunate occurrence ! Poor old Roscoe, he thinks he is quite out of his mind. Hang Mendle ! I wish I had never agreed to help him. It will land me into serious trouble if this is ever found out ! (*enter* MRS. MENDLE, R. I E.) Oh, I'd forgotten all about her !

MRS. M. Get me out of this place at once ; he's seen me !

CULL. *Who's* seen you ?

MRS. M. My hus—Mr. Mendle ! Seen me there ! There ! In your room ! Oh ! what shall I do !

CULL. What the dickens has it got to do with him ?

MRS. M. (*crying*) You don't know ! You don't know ! Oh ! I'm a most unhappy woman ! (*falls on* CULLENDAR'S *shoulder*)

CULL. Oh, I say ! Don't cry ! (*goes to her*) I'm awfully sorry, but after all you are going to be my wife, so what does it matter ? (*puts her in chair,* L. C.)

MRS. M. (*crying*) Oh ! oh ! oh !

CULL. (*kneels*) Hang it, you mustn't cry like this. There, there, there ! (*aside*) It's coming on. (*soothing her, puts arm around her*) There's no harm done. (*aside*) Let me see, I have proposed ? (*aloud*) It was my fault ! I ought not to have asked you to come here. Lydia, bear up. He shan't say anything to you, and if he does, fly to me for protection. (*enter at back,* MENDLE, *followed by* TODDENHAM ; *they listen*) I will shield you with my life, for I love you !

TODD. There, there ! (*aside to* MENDLE) She's carrying on with him now ! I told you what she was. (*comes down* L.)

MENDLE. (C. *Aside*) I can't stand this any longer ! (*comes down, loud cough*)

CULL. (R.) Hallo ! what the devil do you want ? (*bugle ready ; music warning ; curtain warning*)

MENDLE. What right have you to make love to my——

MRS. M. (*pushing* MENDLE *back and taking* C.) Servant ! servant !! Captain Cullendar has as much right to make love to me, as—as you have !

MENDLE. What ? (*sits* L. C., *in despair*)

MRS. M. Yes ! I am only your servant—your poor, ill-used servant—don't forget that. I am free—free to choose whom I like. Captain Cullendar has honored me with his attentions, and I will stand no interference from you or anybody else. (*half crying*) Besides, I'm going to America to-morrow.

TODD. She's a girl of spirit any way. (*bugle call, boot and saddle*)

MENDLE. (*sinks on chair* R. *of table* L.C.) This is the last straw. (*bugle call, " boot and saddle," heard without*)

CULL. Hallo ! what's that ?

Enter ALLISON. *Crosses to* CULL., *salutes.*

ALLIS. (*to* CULLENDAR) We are called out ! The rioters—some thousands strong, have assembled about two miles away, armed, and marching on the town. Police powerless. As the Colonel's ill you must take command.

CULL. (*aside*) Now, I'll pay him out. (*to* MENDLE) Do you hear that, sir ? you must take command !

MENDLE. . Me take command ?

TODD. (*banging on table delightedly*) Take command ! Now is your chance, my boy, charge at the head of your troop—I'll get a four-wheeler and follow you.

CULL. (*to* MENDLE) Do as I tell you, and in the darkness you will escape detection.

MENDLE. (*still sitting*) I'll be hanged if I do ! (*music, piano. " The Minstrel Boy"*)

Enter MIKE, L. C., *stands back of table* L.C.

MIKE. Troop Sergeant Major says the squadron is ready and waiting for you, sir, and the Colonel's horse is ready in the square.

MENDLE. Then let it stop there,—I stop here. (TOD-DENHAM *gets pistol from hook on flat* L.)

CULL. (*aside to* MENDLE) If you don't come I'll tell your stepfather everything.

MENDLE. (*rises*) No! No! Anything but that. I'll come! What's the horse like?

CULL. Quiet as a lamb. (*aside*) It's the one that bolted with Roscoe. (*music little louder.* ALLISON *gives* MENDLE *sword and sabretache,* MENDLE *puts them over his head. Comic business of arming* MENDLE)

MENDLE. (*aside*) There is no escape. (*crosses to* TODD.) Good-bye, I may never see you again. (*aside*) I hope to goodness I never shall! (*aloud*) Farewell, everybody—farewell. (*to* MRS. M.) But as for you, false woman! sending me to my death, if ever I come back I'll—I'll——

TODD. (*who has taken horse-pistol from the wall and offers it to* MENDLE) That's right, my boy—draw your sword and wave it over your head. (*by this time* ALLISON *and* CULLENDAR *are standing either side door, back, swords drawn and holding them at " the salute,"* MRS. MENDLE *shrinking at door* R., MIKE *at window, back*)

MENDLE. (*draws sword and sweeps the stage*) Rather! my country calls! (*bus. with sword, etc.*) Mendle to the rescue! Death or glory or both—now to do or—don't! Lead on! (*heroically*) Captain Cullendar, if I fall—pick me up! (*exit* L. C., ROSCOE *rushes from the room—just in time to see* MENDLE'S *back—shouting " Hi! hi! you!"* TODDENHAM *catches him by bath robe.* ROSCOE *falls, and* TODDENHAM *presents wrong end of pistol at him, saying, as curtain falls,* " *Here, where the devil are you going to!* "

CURTAIN.

ACT III.

SCENE.—*Same as Act* I. *Stage partly dark—blind down, etc. ready for bell*

Enter MARTHA, *pulls blind up, blows out candle, goes to door* R., *looks in.*

MARTHA. Master not at home, Missis ditto, and a nice night I've had all alone, with myself and the cat, and not a 'a'porth of consolation. Mike didn't turn up, and I had to go to my sister's after all. (*bell rings, starts*) Lor' save us, I'm that nervous I ain't got a bit of nerve left. (*exits* L. C. *and re-enters* L. C. *with* MIKE) You're a nice cup of tea, you are !

MIKE. Cup of tea ! I am the dregs and no sugar. There's the devil and all to pay.

MARTHA. Where were you last night, MAN ?

MIKE. Ah, niver moind *me*. Where's your master, has he come home ?

MARTHA. No, he has not.

MIKE. Is his Missus at home ?

MARTHA. No, she is not.

MIKE. Phew ! There'll be murdher done this day.

MARTHA. Why didn't you meet me last night ?

MIKE. (*bus. backing her to corner*) Ye Cleopathra. Meet ye, is it ? Yer—yer Cleopathra. Why do you decave the sivin senses of me when all along you know you're going to marry another blackguard.

MARTHA. Mike, you've been drinking.

MIKE. Drinkin' is it ! Faith no ! but I'll take to it from this hour. I suppose you couldn't keep yer hands off the title. Mrs. Captain Cullendar sounds mighty foine, doesn't it ?

MARTHA. What is all this you've got into your head ? Who told you I was going to marry Cullendar ?

MIKE. Didn't I hear him with me own blessed ears tell the Liftinint so. He said he was going to marry Mendle's servant. (*the truth dawning upon* MARTHA, *she bursts out laughing.* MIKE *imitates her*)

MARTHA. (L. C.) Oh, you worm, you blind wriggly worm ! Can't you see it's not me—it's missis. (*laughs*)

Here's a mess! The Captain has fallen in love with the missis—oh, the artful one ! she's eloped with your master of course.

MIKE. Divil a bit, he's in his quarters this blessed minute.

MARTHA. Then he's not run away.

MIKE. Run away is it ? What ! after the fight ?

MARTHA. I can't make it out at all. Any way, Mike, I'm not going to marry anyone but you.

MIKE. Saints alive ! say that wanst more and I'll die happy.

MARTHA. Better *live* happy instead.

MIKE. Hurroo ! me angel ! Forgive me calling ye Cleopathra just now, and make it all up wid a kiss. (*bus.*) But heaven forgive me, I'm forgetting what I came here for, and it's a nice mess I've got ye all into. The Colonel, Colonel Roscoe, the bloodthirsty old Saxon, got wind of the matter and sends for me this morning. Ses he : " My man, you're in this affair and if ye don't tell me the whole truth of it I'll coort martial the whole lot, and probably hang one or two of you. Well, you see, me darlin', as I was mad with the Captain by rayson of him marrying you, I told the Colonel the most of the matther, and he's coming here for an explanation.

MARTHA. But where *is* master ! Perhaps he's shot. (*noise of key ready*)

MIKE. Och, divil a bit ! He'd sooner *die* first. Well, if he should turn up, keep him out of the way. (*goes up* L. C.) I'll be off back or I'll be missed. Good-bye, me colleen, they may shoot the whole brigade, meself included, so long as you'll marry me afther. (*exit door in flat* L. C.)

MARTHA. As Mike says, a pretty mess indeed. But the idea of Captain Cullendar wanting to marry Mrs. Mendle is delightful. I knew something of that sort would happen sooner or later. (*noise of key in lock*) Master ! (*enter* MRS. MENDLE, *door in flat, looking ill and rather untidy*) No ! Missis ! (MARTHA *takes her cloak off, puts it on chair* L. C.)

MRS. M. (*sinks into a chair* R. C.) Martha, get me a cup of tea.

MARTHA. Have something stronger than tea—do, mum, you do look awful !

MRS. M. (*staring at the floor*) I am awful—I'm an awful woman. I'm—I'm a murderess.

MARTHA. Lor, mum !

MRS. M. (*crying*) I have sent that poor dear forth to his death.

MARTHA. Master ? (*at back of table*)

MRS. M. Your master. He fell fighting ! He must have fallen fighting or he would now be home. He would never miss his morning cup of tea.

MARTHA. But how do you know he's fallen fighting. (*crosses to* R.)

MRS. M. (*to* MARTHA) Instinct. Unerring instinct. The instinct of a widow.

MARTHA. Well, then, it doesn't much matter.

MRS. M. (*indignantly*) Doesn't much matter !

MARTHA. Well, mum, if he's dead he's dead, and it'll save him being killed by somebody else.

MRS. M. What do you mean ?

MARTHA. (*crosses to* C.) I mean they are searching for him everywhere.

MRS. M. So have *I* been—all night—his mangled body always before me. (*She keeps her eyes continually in one spot as though she saw* MENDLE'S *body.*) But who— who else is searching for him ?

MARTHA. (*crosses to table*) I don't rightly understand it all, but Mike—you remember Mike, mum ?—he's been here to say that the Colonel has found out everything and is searching everywhere for master, and swearing he will kill him.

MRS. M. Oh, dear, oh, dear, this is worse and worse !

MARTHA. Shall I go for the police, mum ? (*at sideboard*)

MRS. M. (*rises*) No ! don't leave me ; we will go together. (*crossing to* L.) Stay ! Lock all the doors, especially my poor dear departed's. It's all my fault ; it's all my wicked, deceitful nature ! Ah, if I ever get out of this and poor Monty is still alive, I'll reform, I will indeed——

MARTHA. (*who brings down wine glass with brandy*) Here, mum, do take this, it'll do you good. (*music and warning crash ready*)

MRS. M. Thank you. (*takes glass*) Now, Martha, we will go and see if we cannot obtain some protection from this colonel man ; and now I come to think of it, we may as well give the police some description of the (*shudders*) body. (*exeunt*, L. C.)

After a pause a sound as of breaking wood and glass, then a groan, and enter MENDLE, L. ; *he is dressed in a suit half military, half Irish peasant, is much dilapidated, very pale, and carries a big shillalah. He staggers down front. At* MENDLE'S *entrance the band plays tremolo, " Home Sweet Home !"*

MENDLE. Home at last ! Home, sweet home. Be it ever so difficult to get into, there's no place like home. No latch'key ; had to break into the kitchen at the back. Where is everybody ? Where is Martha ? Where is Lydia ? Lydia ! Lydia ! (*goes to door of bedroom and knocks loudly*) She's not there, not there ! She's not been home all night. Then it's true ; she's left me—left me for that soldier. Oh, Lydia, how could you ? What is he to you that I am not ? Look at us both. Am I not his superior in everything but (*looking down at himself*) personal appearance ? (*sneezes*) What a cold I've caught, and I'm so stiff I can hardly move. (*tries to sit*). That saddle must have been made of cast iron. (*writhes*) The moment we quitted the barracks, we broke into a trot—I broke into a perspiration ! Lost a stirrup—bumped all over one side. Cullendar put me straight—nearly went over on the other. On and on—battledore and shuttlecock. *I* was the shuttlecock. And then we cantered, at least the horse did ; I still trotted. If they would only stop ! Oh, the agonizing pain ! Still they went on. At least we reached a huge crowd, shouting, swearing, cursing, and flinging stones—silly habit throwing stones—one hit my beast, he rose up in the air like a rocking horse, and when he came down again, I'd slipped over his tail. I managed to get clear of the crowd, crawled under a bush, and laid down aching in every limb. Then the firing commenced, so did the rain. I was there hours, wet through, clothes in ribbons, and no hat. The riot was over, soldiers gone, and I started to stagger home. On the way I hid the upper part of my uniform, got these clothes, such as they are, off a scarecrow in a field. Home at last, to find it ruined and deserted. (*sneezes*) I think I'll go and change these beastly clothes, and try and get dry again. (*goes to door, R. 1 E. ; finds it locked*) Of course ! Locked ! That's clever, that is, of Mrs. Mendle. (*goes to window*) Thank goodness, here's Martha, but who's she got with her ? Looks like a police inspector. (*door heard opening;*

MENDLE *makes a final effort to open door of his room*)
No go! (*rushes to table, and, sitting, tries to appear un-
concerned ; whistles faintly and thrums on the table
with his fingers*)

MARTHA. (*outside*) I tell you my master is not at
home.

Enter COLONEL ROSCOE *and* MARTHA, *door in flat.*

ROSCOE. Private O'Docherty, remain outside till I call.
It's useless ! Silence ! Don't dare to answer me. This
is Mendle's den, and I'll beard the brute in it. (*doesn't
see* MENDLE. MARTHA *utters exclamation of terror at seeing* MENDLE. MENDLE *makes movements suggesting that*
MARTHA *is to go.* ROSCOE *turns quickly.*) What's that ?
(*sees* MENDLE) Ha ! Who's this ? Hi, you ! (*hits the
table with his stick. Stands* R. *of table* R. C.)

MENDLE. (*picks up his hat ; gives it to* MARTHA)
Hang my hat in the hall. (*exit* MARTHA, L. C.)

ROSCOE. (MENDLE *never stirs*) Who are you ?
Where's Mendle ?

MENDLE. (*aside*) Doesn't know me. (*aloud*) Beg
pardon ?

ROSCOE. (R.) I say, who—are—you—and—where—is
—Mendle ?

MENDLE. Oh, certainly ! (*imitating*) Who—are—
you——

ROSCOE. My name's Roscoe, Colonel Roscoe.

MENDLE. Great heavens, and I've got his trousers on !
(*pulls tablecloth over his trousers*)

ROSCOE. Are you deaf, dumb, or an idiot ? Speak,
man, where is Mendle ?

MENDLE. He's—er—er—out.

ROSCOE. Don't lie to me. Who are you ?

MENDLE. I—I—oh, I'm—er—the man in possession.

ROSCOE. You look it. In possession of what ?

MENDLE. Oh, all this. (*waves hand idiotically*)

ROSCOE. I'm ill. Where's the brandy ? (*sits* R.)

MENDLE. In the cellarette—I mean—I should say—it
was on the sideboard.

ROSCOE. Then ring the bell for some one to get it,
quick.

MENDLE. About to rise. (*aside*) I daren't get up.
(*aloud*) The bell is on your side.

ROSCOE. Damned impertinence. (*gets up, rings bell*)
Is Mendle a bankrupt ?

MENDLE. Hasn't got a penny. (*enter* MARTHA, L. C.)
Martha, brandy.

ROSCOE. How do you know her name's Martha.

MENDLE. Heard them call her Martha, so I thought
it was her name. Your name is Martha, isn't it, Martha ?

ROSCOE. (*suspiciously*) Oh !

MENDLE. This gentleman wants some brandy.

ROSCOE. (*turning suddenly to* MARTHA) Where's
your master ?   Where's your master ?

MARTHA. There. (*points to* MENDLE. MENDLE
makes signs. MARTHA *gets brandy*)

ROSCOE. What,--*that ?*

MENDLE. This, certainly ! I'm master here, master
of the master, master of the entire establishment, so if I
allow you some brandy, you're drinking the creditors'
money.

MARTHA *places brandy on table and one glass near the*
COLONEL—*then takes out key, unlocks door* L., *and
exits. As* MENDLE *has the tablecloth over his legs,*
MARTHA *puts it straight before setting down the decanter. This uncovers* MENDLE's *legs so that after
the* COLONEL *has sipped the brandy* MENDLE *gradually draws the tablecloth towards him, the* COLONEL
*not noticing until he wants his glass, and then sees it
more than half across the table. During dialogue
this is repeated three times.*

ROSCOE. You're very kind—my heart is affected ; must
have brandy, don't mind whose (*sips*) not at all bad—
quite decent.

MENDLE. (L. *of table*) It ought to be, cost me ninety-
six shillings a dozen.

ROSCOE. (R. *of table*) What ?

MENDLE. I say it must have cost ninety-six shillings a
dozen.

ROSCOE. How on earth should you know ! (MENDLE
puts finger to nose, and jerks his thumb in direction of
MARTHA) Oh, I see ! Well, I'm not sorry this man
Mendle is in trouble—he's a scoundrel. One can't kill a
man like that.

MENDLE. Thank goodness ! (*aside*)

ROSCOE. But one *can* horsewhip him within an inch

of killing him, and that's what I'm here to do. (*feels for glass, finds that* MENDLE *has dragged it with the cloth to his side of the table*) What the devil are you doing with the tablecloth. (*uncovers* MENDLE)

MENDLE. Er—oh—nothing.

ROSCOE. (*pulls back cloth*—MENDLE *shoots legs under table*) Then sit still, can't you ? It won't be my fault if *he* ever sits or walks again.

MENDLE. (*aside*) Oh, my poor wife ! (*drags cloth back*)

ROSCOE. (*very loudly and bringing his hand violently down on table*) And by the bones of the Commander-in-chief and the ashes of the War Office—if he doesn't turn up in five minutes I'll call in my orderly and wreck the place.

MENDLE. Good heavens ! (*laughs hysterically*) Ha, ha, very funny, very ludicrous, very——

ROSCOE. (*very loudly*) Don't laugh ! don't laugh ! or by the heaven I'll practice on you till he does come. Do you think I'm to be fooled, trifled with and insulted by a little dirty sneak of a thieving lawyer ! You're mistaken—you shall stop here and see for yourself. (*cloth bus. repeated ; this time, however, the* COLONEL *removes decanter, etc., pulls the cloth off the table and rolls it up and sits on it*)

MENDLE. Puts his legs under the table. (*aside*) It's all over, I'm lost.

ROSCOE. (*pulls out his watch*) Now I'll give him five minutes exactly ; at the end of that time—(*pushes decanter and glass towards* MENDLE ; *then pulls it back again*) well—you'll see.

MENDLE. (*plucking up*) Now look here, you know you can't do anything of the kind. I'm in possession here, and this stuff belongs to his creditors, and I warn you if you attempt any violence, (*unthinkingly rises*) I say if you——

ROSCOE. (*rises*) Hello, why, where the devil did you get those overalls ? (*pointing to trousers*)

MENDLE. (*in extreme terror, going back* L.) Overalls ? I haven't got any overalls—I mean I——

Enter MRS. MENDLE, L. C., *suddenly sees* MENDLE, *utters a loud exclamation, and nearly faints on floor*)

MRS. M. (R.) Monty !

MENDLE. (L. C.) Saved !

ROSCOE. (R. *turns upon her*) What's that ? What do you want—who are you ?

MRS. M. I'm the *General*—

ROSCOE. The what ?

MRS. M. (C.) The General. The—the general servant.

ROSCOE. Oh ! (*aside*) She's a devilish stylish woman. No wonder, with all these good-looking women about, Mendle's a bankrupt.

MRS. M. Who said Mendle is a bankrupt ?

ROSCOE. That man with those—where *did* you get those overalls ?

MENDLE. What overalls ? (*walks up* C., *stooping down, so that the tail of his coat hides his legs*)

ROSCOE. That restless fidgety tablecloth-dragging idiot. Ah, that reminds me—put this out of his way. (*hands cloth. Seeing* MRS. M.'s *white hands and rings*) Hello ! Gad, eh ! general servant ! Hand like that—fifty guinea diamond ring. This is not a servant's hand—here's a mare's nest—this is no place for me ! (*calls* O'DOCHERTY. *Puts tablecloth in his pocket. Enter* O'DOCHERTY *in door flat* L. C.) O'Docherty ! (*going up* C.) remain here, keep your eye on that man till I return. This must be seen to. (*going off, throws tablecloth at* MARTHA. *Exit fussily* L. C., *saying " I'll sift this to the bottom," etc.*)

MIKE. Be the bones av me ancesthors, I'm in a nice hole betwixt 'em !

MENDLE. (*with assumed dignity*) Martha, leave the room and take that wild Scotchman with you. (*crossing down* L. MARTHA *goes to door, beckons* MIKE, *who is at first resolute.* MARTHA, *by action, commands.* MIKE *wheels half round and follows* MARTHA *at quick march. When they exit* MENDLE *folds his arms and confronts* MRS. M. MRS. M. *does the same*) Mrs. Mendle !

MRS. M. (R. C.) Mr. Mendle !

MENDLE. (L. C.) Aren't you ashamed to look me in the face ?

MRS. M. Aren't you ashamed to look *me* in the face ?

MENDLE. Good heavens ! what have I done ? Haven't I suffered enough ?

MRS. M. And do you think I have not suffered ?

MENDLE. You—ha, ha ! (*hysterically*)

MRS. M. I—do you think that when the Colonel's horse came back with an empty saddle we were going to leave you to perish ? No ! we formed a search party to find you, dead or alive.

MENDLE. After what I saw, Madam, I should imagine my mangled corpse would have been a *lucky find.*

MRS. M. Oh, the ingratitude of men ! (*goes up* L.)

MENDLE. Oh, the perfidy of women ! (*goes up* R.)

MRS. M. How dare you ! (*coming* C.)

MENDLE. (*coming* C.) Dare ? Look what I have dared these twelve hours, and all for you, and how am I repaid ?

MRS. M. What do you mean ?

MENDLE. Ask Captain Cullendar.

MRS. M. Wretch ! (*goes to door* L.)

MENDLE. Woman ! (*goes to door* R., *finds it locked.*)

MRS. M. Brute ! here is the key of your den. (*throws key across stage*) Go in and gnaw the meatless bones of remorse—I'll never speak to you again. (*throws key, hits him on the nose. Exit* L. 2 E., *banging door*)

MENDLE. (*hysterically*) Go on, go on ! I'm quite beginning to like it. (*row outside.* TODD. *is shot onto stage, followed at the same moment by* O'D. *and* MARTHA. MENDLE *rushes at door* L. *Bursts it open and exits*)

ROSCOE. (L. C.) Sit there, sir, and stir at your peril. So "I'm a drivelling lunatic at large, eh ?" P'raps so ! but lunatics are dangerous, as you shall find. (*bus.*)

TODD. (*sits. Mildly*) My dear sir, I'm so sorry to find you no better. I was in hopes a night's rest would set you up.

ROSCOE. I'll set *you* up, my friend, and have you shot.

TODD. (*aside*) He's decidedly worse. (*turning to* MIKE) See here, my man, I suppose you're paid for looking after this poor thing ; then why don't you do it ?

ROSCOE. Damn it, sir, I——

TODD. (*in chair* L. C. *of table ; to* MIKE) There he goes ! He'll do himself or someone else an injury, and then you'll be responsible for it ; take him away.

ROSCOE. This is beyond forbearance. Now attend to me, Mr. Spindle, Windle, or Mindle—whatever your blackguardly name may be. (*turns suddenly to* MIKE) Isn't that the ruffian's name ? Mindle, Windle ? (MIKE *in bewilderment ;* TODD. *crosses to* R. *as* ROSCOE *comes to him*)

MARTHA. (*aside to* MIKE) Say yes, or it's all over between us.

ROSCOE. Do you hear me ?

MIKE. It is, sir ! Mindle !

ROSCOE. Very good. Now, Mindle, I am tossing up in my mind whether to break every bone in your body or hand you over to the police. You stand convicted of theft, and with defacing and degrading Her Majesty's uniform ! You must be imprisoned. A fine won't do, as you are already a bankrupt with a man in possession. (*coming* C.)

TODD. (*to* MIKE) I say, don't you carry something about you to give him when he's like this ?

ROSCOE. Silence, you—you—worm! (TODDENHAM *picks up decanter by the neck, threatens* ROSCOE *with it, holding it upside down. The brandy appears to run down* TODDENHAM'S *sleeve*) Now, out of consideration for you age and general half-witted appearance, I give you your choice. Will you go quietly to the police station with this man, (*pointing to* MIKE) or would you prefer the police and a stretcher ? I give you sixteen seconds and a half to determine. (*pulls out watch*)

MARTHA. (*to* MIKE—*aside*) Take him away and the master is saved.

TODD. (*aside*, R.) Brilliant notion. I will go with him to the station, and when I get him there, I'll charge him with being a lunatic at large.

ROSCOE. Time's up.

TODD. I'll go ! (*laughing, going up* C.)

ROSCOE. Private O'Docherty, conduct that man to the police station.

TODD. (*still laughing—aside to* O'D.) It's wonderful how very easily managed these lunatics are, after all.

ROSCOE. About turn—quick march. (O'D. *passes his arm through* TODD.'S, *and swings him off* C. *to* R., *followed by* ROSCOE)

MARTHA. Mike's as handy a boy with his feet as any man betwixt here and Galway. Good luck to him. (*bell.* MARTHA *answers the door*)

Re-enter MARTHA, MRS. MORRISON *and* GERALDINE.

MRS. MOR. Very unbusinesslike not to be in in business hours.

MARTHA. I didn't say he was out ; I said I'd see if he was in.

MRS. MOR. (*hands card*) Same thing. My card! Say important business, but won't detain him ten minutes.

MARTHA. Yes, ma'am. (*exit door* R.)

GERALD. (*down* L.) Don't you think all this fuss about me is quite unnecessary?

MRS. MOR. With any sensible minded girl—yes! But you with all your obstinacy and unbusinesslike ways—no! I must know exactly where I am.

GERALD. Well! If *your* business notions overrule your good taste and pride, *mine* do not, and I'm not going to marry a man who has refused me.

MRS. MOR. Now you are talking business. You well know if you don't marry Mr. Allison you lose your fortune, and I must know how the money is to be disposed of legally.

GERALD. Dispose of the money as you like, but I won't be disposed of with it, so there!

MRS. MOR. Dear! dear! She will never learn business.

Enter MARTHA, R.

MARTHA. Mr. Mendle will be with ye in a minute, mum. (*aside*) Poor master, his hand trembled so I had to button his collar for him. (*crosses to* L., *exits* L. C.)

Enter MENDLE, R. I E. *He has a preoccupied air.*

MENDLE. (*crosses down* L.) Good-morning. Can I be of any use to you? (*crosses to* C. *Aside*) My head is spinning. (*shakes hands mechanically in the air*)

MRS. MOR. You are a lawyer?

MENDLE. Am I—I'm not absolutely certain this morning.

MRS. MOR. I beg your pardon?

MENDLE. (R.) I mean my head is marching up and down, retiring by sections, forming squares——

MRS. MOR. Sir!

MENDLE. I can't help it, I've got a military case—uniform case—a case of overalls. I mean I must over-all your case—excuse me—state *your* case, it may steady me.

MRS. MOR. You remember our conversation yesterday?

MENDLE. Perfectly. About what? (*bell ready*)

MRS. MOR. Marriage settlements. This young lady's fortune and so on.

MENDLE. Oh, yes—ah—of course. (*aside*) Haven't the faintest idea what she's talking about.

MRS. MOR. Well, the whole position's changed.

MENDLE. (*mechanically*) About turn. (*bell*)

MRS. MOR. Exactly! now she absolutely refuses to obey orders.

MENDLE. Call out a file—seven days cells.

MRS. MOR. Cells? File?

MENDLE. Eh? Oh, ah! (*laughs feebly*) Cells—pigeon holes, files, gimlet's, next room, files, papers.

MARTHA *enters and crosses to* R.

MARTHA. (*hands a blue official looking paper to* MENDLE) P'leeceman. (*suddenly holding the paper under his nose*)

MENDLE. (*half aside*) I'm ready! I'll go quietly. (*buttons up his coat*)

MARTHA. Waiting answer.

MENDLE. (*to* MRS. MOR.) Oh, I thought—excuse me! (*opens letter,* MRS. MOR. *joins daughter at back. As he glances through letter, face distorted, he reads at intervals with a gasp*) "From the Police Headquarters to landlady, No. 12 Shannon St. If you haven't found my son's body, come yourself at once—am given in charge by Roscoe. Something about stolen uniform, bail refused. Toddenham." This is the final blow—the last straw—Wife gone, fortune gone, practice gone, an avalanche of retribution has fallen upon me. (*sits* L. C. *Places letter on table* L., *where it is left*)

MARTHA. Any answer, sir?

MENDLE. Of course there's an answer, I always answer answers. (*writes*) "Mendle's body recovered, it will be with you directly." (*blots letter on edge of table, tears it in half, throws it on the ground, turns to* MARTHA) Well, what are you waiting for?

MARTHA. The letter.

MENDLE. Where is it?

MARTHA. On the floor, sir!

MENDLE. (*picks it up*) Silly girl, throwing things about like that. (*writes the address on his knee, tears it in half and gives it to* MARTHA. *Exit* MARTHA) I say, Martha, say I'm out, I will not be bothered by a pack of silly women. (*sees* MRS. MORRISON, *rises and goes to* GERALDINE) How are you ? What can I do for you ?

GERALD. Ma's come about the will. (*stands* L. *of table* L. C.)

MENDLE. Oh, ah ! (*goes to* MRS. MOR. *and pulls at the bag she carries as though it were a bell rope*) Martha—oh, beg pardon, thought it was the bell. My dear Madam—I must look over the copy of the will once more before I can finally decide to give my final decision.

MRS. MOR. I have a copy with me.

MENDLE. Then come into the barracks—I mean office. I must have a court martial—I mean I must martial your case into court. There's no one there, my dear. My clerk is playing soldiers with another head clerk—I mean this way—(*pushes* MRS. MOR. *off* L., *bangs against* GERALDINE) this way. (*pushes her off. Exit* I E. L).

Re-enter MARTHA, L.

MARTHA. Everything is going that contrary-wise I don't know w'ether I'm on my head or my heels. I must look after poor missis though. (*going, stops*) It strikes me I've left that street door open. I can't help it if I have. (*exit* L. 2 E.)

Enter CAPTAIN CULLENDAR *and* ALLISON, L. C.—ALLISON *still very dejected. Enter door in flat* R.

CULL. (R. C.) My dear fellow, I'm sorry to trespass on your good nature, but I must enlist your aid in this matter. Roscoe has got wind of the affair, and goodness only knows how it will end.

ALLIS. (L. C.) My dear boy, I'm in that state of mind I don't care what you do with me. What do you propose ?

CULL. (R. C.) This man Mendle must be got out of the way; if he meets Roscoe the fat will be in the fire to that extent it may cost me my commission.

ALLIS. You don't want me to murder him ? I feel I'm desperate enough even for that. (*goes* L., *sits* L. C.)

CULL. (*sits* R. C.) What's the trouble, old man ?

ALLIS. What's the trouble with every man ? A woman. A doocid deceitful, dear, delightful woman !

CULL. (*rises*) Shake ! (*holds out hand ; business*) Her name should be Dorothy, and the alliteration is perfect.

5

ALLIS. Don't chaff, old chap, or I shall cry. I'm a fool, an ass, an idiot. I've refused one of the most dangerous——

CULL. Another D.

ALLIS. Of her sex.

Enter GERALDINE, *unseen*, L. I E., *remains* C. *at back. Goes up* L.

GERALD. I cannot stand that miserable law jargon any longer.

ALLIS. I've refused *one*——

CULL. And I've accepted one.

ALLIS. (*rises, crosses to* CULL.)   Shake ! (*bus. as before*)

CULL. But I'm going to cry off!

ALLIS. And I'm going to cry *on !* What's up ?

CULL. Just this. My beastly complaint came back again yesterday. I've seen Geraldine, and I can't live without her.

ALLIS. I'll take devilish good care you don't live with her. I'm going to ask her to make it up and marry me as per orders.

CULL. Rubbish ! You have put yourself out of court with *that* lady !

GERALD. (C. *Coming forward*) Then I'll be the usher and call Archie Allison back into court.

ALLIS. Geraldine—you—you mean it ?

GERALD. Yes ! oh ! it's not your merit, sir ! It's merely to put an end to those horrid law proceedings in there. (*points off*)

CULL. I protest ! This lady's hand——

ALLIS. Hand ? it's only a finger. This one (*holds up* GERALDINE'S *left hand and points to the third finger*)

GERALD. Do you swear to obey that finger ?

ALLIS. Yes, after you have sworn to obey me ! Let us go and buy a ring to fit it and bind the bargain, shall we ?

GERALD. Certainly.

ALLIS. What about Cullendar ?

GERALD. He shall be your best man ! Ta, ta !

ALLIS. Bye-bye. (*exeunt* ALLISON *and* GERALDINE, L. C.)

CULL. (*after looking after them some few seconds,*

scratches his nose in a thoughtful way) Damn ! (*turns and sees* MRS. MENDLE, *who has entered* L. 2 E.)

MRS. M. Captain Cullendar ! this is fortunate !

CULL. (*sees* MRS. M.'S *changed costume*) Ah ! This is the Lydia I used to know ! Ah ! any news of our friend ?

MRS. M. He has turned up.

CULL. That's lucky. I must see him—urgent business. Is he in the house ?

MRS. M. I really don't know. His business has ceased to interest me.

CULL. But my business concerns you.

MRS. M. In what way ?

CULL. When I consulted Mendle about your damages, you know his advice ? Well, I've tried hard to act on it. I can't. I've seen her again.

MRS. M. Her—who ?

CULL. Miss Morrison, and I can't do it. I don't know whether you can bring a second action for damages, as the other isn't paid ; but I'll raise the money somehow, pay the first like a man, and I hope you'll think none the worse of me.

MRS. M. (*smiling to herself*) Thank you—but—in any case I could not entertain your generous offer, as I have been married these six months. There ! the murder's out.

CULL. (*drops into chair*, R. C. MRS. M. *walks over to table where* TODD.'S *letter is*) What—to—? I mean whom to ?

MRS. M. Mrs. Mendle, at your service. (*curtseys. A table* L.)

CULL. (*sits* R. C. *Aside*) Good heavens !—dodged bigamy by a hair's breadth. I see, Mendle knows nothing about your being the plaintiff in our breach of promise.

MRS. M. Precisely. (*has found and is reading* TODD'S *letter*)

CULL. Oh, woman, woman !

MRS. M. Gracious heavens ! (*rings bell on table* L. C.)

CULL. (*jumping up, crosses to her*) what's broken loose now !

MRS. M. (*crosses to* C.) Read ! (*hands letter*) must see my husband at once. (*enter* MARTHA, L. C. How long has this letter been here ?

MARTHA. Two or three minutes, mum. P'leeceman.

MRS. M. Where's your master ?

MARTHA. In the office. (*exit* L. 2 E.)

MRS. M. (*aside*) Heavens ! Toddenham in prison !
He'll never catch the boat to-morrow. Captain Cullendar,
ask no questions ! Go to the police station bail that man
out, and I'll never mention damages again. (CULL. *without a word snatches hat up and bolts off door back
to* R.)

Enter MENDLE, L. I E., *he does not see* MRS. M.

MENDLE. (C.) I've given that business woman something to keep her quiet for a time. (*sees* MRS. M.)

MRS. M. (R. C.) I hope you're satisfied with your
work.

MENDLE. Quite ! but I'm dissatisfied with yours.

MRS. M. You've brought things to a pretty pass.
(*holds out letter*) He, the monster, is in jail !

MENDLE. I know it, I'm going to bail him out.

MRS. M. Spare yourself the trouble. Captain Cullendar——

MENDLE. (*coming down* C.) How dare you mention
his name to me !

MRS. M. Pray, why not ? (*bell ready*)

MENDLE. Have you forgotten the disgraceful scene I
witnessed yesterday ?

MRS. M. For goodness' sake, Mendle, don't make a
fool of yourself. Whatever I did was entirely for you and
for the best.

MENDLE. Really ? Still I am entitled to a full explanation.

MRS. M. You shall have it, but not now.

MENDLE. Does he know I'm safe ?

MRS. M. He knows nothing, unless *you* told him.

MENDLE. I merely sent word to say " Mendle's body
recovered." (*bell*)

MRS. M. Good ! (*crosses* L.) Leave him to me.
(*goes up to window*) Here he is ; go back into your
room and lie down.

MENDLE. But—Captain—Cul——

MRS. M. Trust to me. (*she whispers in his ear ; he
nods as though pleased ; she pushes him off then rushes
off herself and puts on cap and apron*)

Enter TODD *and* CULLENDAR, L. C.

TODD. (*down* R. C.) The awkward part was when we got to the station. That wild Indian gave *me* in charge. What is your advice?

CULL. (C.) As you are sure to get the worst of it, my advice is bolt! Never mind the bail.

TODD. No. Before I go I must know my poor dear boy's fate. (*enter* MRS. M. *in cap and apron from* 2 E. L.) Ah! now we shall learn something. Well, young woman, what news?

MRS. M. Alas, sir!

TODD. (*breaking in*) I knew it, I knew it. I'm his murderer. Take me back to prison. It's all I'm fit for.

MRS. M. But, sir—I——

TODD. Don't speak to me. He's dead. (*turns to* CULL.) and partly your doing. He should have been properly guarded and not allowed to risk his precious life. (*half crying*)

CULL. There was no holding him on—I mean no holding him back. When danger threatened he was all there.

TODD. And now he's all where? (*sits* R. C.)

CULL. I should not like to suggest.

MRS. M. (*aside to* CULL.) Go into the office and leave him to me.

CULL. (*aside to* MRS. M.) Get him to bolt. I'll pay his bail as a fine for my conduct to you. (*crosses* L. *Exit into office,* I E. L.).

MRS. M. (*cries*) Mr. Toddenham, may I speak to you?

TODD. (*crying*) Talk away, young woman—nothing can alter the present or recall the past. It's all my doing. I forced him into that terrible profession. If he were alive, I'd make him give it up, resign, get blackballed, pilled, or whatever they do.

MRS. M. You really mean it? (TODD. *nods emphatically*) But is he really dead?

TODD. (*hands paper*) Look at that, " Mendle's body recovered." Where is it? What does it look like? I'll see, it even if it is covered with wounds, back and front.

MRS. M. It's in there. (*points off* R.)

TODD. (*hesitating*) In there! all of it! No, I can't do it. My nerve is not what it used to be. (*crosses to* L.)

MRS. M. (*with melodramatic voice*) Well! if you won't go to the body, I must bring the body to you. (*exit into* MENDLE'S *room*, R. 1 E.

TODD. Poor fellow! (*goes* L., *and sits at table.* So young and promising. (*enter* MR. *and* MRS. MENDLE. MENDLE *carries his arm in a sling, and has his head and one foot ridiculously bound up in linen bandages, and uses a housemaid's broom as a crutch*) My brave soldier boy——(*going to him.* MENDLE *shrinks*) My hero!

MRS. M. Don't touch him!

TODD. Thank heaven you are alive!

MENDLE. (C. *In a weak voice*) Only just. But I've had a narrow escape.

TODD. You shall give up soldiering. I won't run another such a risk. I will remain in England, and we will all settle down together.

MENDLE. But how about America?

TODD. (*aside*) Now comes my turn. America! I'm not going.

MRS. M. *and* MENDLE. Not going!

TODD. No, the fact of it is that in my anxiety about you I clean forgot my own troubles. You see before you a—a—pauper.

MRS. M. *and* MENDLE. A what? (MENDLE *drops broom;* MRS. M. *fixes it under wrong arm*)

TODD. A pauper, a ruined man—but what of that, since you are safe—I don't complain.

MRS. M. *and* MENDLE. Com-plain! But what about him?)
me? }

TODD. My boy, you're no worse off,—you'll only have to work.

MRS. M. *and* MENDLE. Work!

TODD. Yes, work! work! Don't glare at me like that; it's worse for me than for you (*sinks in chair* R. *of table* R. C.)

MRS. M. Worse, and we have had all this deceit and trouble for nothing.

MENDLE. (*using broom as a stick*) Lydia, if there are any knives in this room, remove them. Look at that placid idiot. He has given us twenty-four hours of acute misery. He has caused us to lay in a stock of lies that would have made even Ananias blush. He has caused us to descend to lying, deceit, and crime; and there he sits, the keystone of this colossal fabric of subterfuge, there I say, he sits—and lives !

TODD. Consider, my dear boy, it's not my fault. So long as I had it you never wanted.

MRS. M. That's true, Monty ; remember that.

MENDLE. I do, (*throws away broom*) and that's why I'll have no more of this hypocrisy, lying, and subterfuge. Lydia, off with your subterfuge. (LYDIA *takes cap and apron off*) Sir, behold my wife !

TODD. (*surprised*) And I nearly eloped with her.

MENDLE. And myself, Montague Mendle, solicitor, commissioner of oaths, etc., 22 Shannon Street. (*tears off bandages*) There, the murder's out !

TODD. That's all very well, my dear boy, but what about your commission ? What about the army ?

MENDLE. Army ! If you haven't had enough of the army, I have, and in future I'll never lead anything more ferocious than a blind puppy. (*music, and curtain warning*)

TODD. Well, perhaps it's for the best, after all, because I've got a capital idea. If I could only get some sharp, clever lawyer to run over to New York, I believe enough might be saved out of the estate to make us all three comfortable.

MRS. M. (*pointing to* MENDLE) Here's your very man.

TODD. The solicitor—of course !

MENDLE. (*extending both hands to* TODD.) Then we are forgiven?

TODD. Why certainly ! (*curtain. Music pp.*)

Enter MRS. MOR. *and* GER., L. I E. *followed by* O'D. *and* MARTHA *from* C.

O'D. (*extreme* R., *saluting*) Colonel Roscoe has come home, sor, in a high state of fever, gone to bed and sent for the doctor ; and Mr. Allison says will you return to barracks at once. (*goes back to* MARTHA. CULLENDAR *makes movement as though to bolt.* MRS. M. *affectionately detains him*)

MRS. M. More business, Mendle ! marriage settlement in the matter of Captain Cecil Cullendar and Amelia Morrison, Widow.

CULL. Yes. Came on quite suddenly ! Hope it won't go off as suddenly.

TODD. More business, my boy !

MENDLE. Right! Give me good old parchment, wigs, and red tape. Lydia! Attention! Left half turn, present arms, embrace! (LYDIA *embraces* MENDLE, *giving her* R. *hand to* TODD., *over* MENDLE'S *shoulder, who bends over it.* CULLENDAR *and* MORRISON *ditto.* MIKE *and* MARTHA *embrace at back.*)

CURTAIN.

www.ingramcontent.com/pod-product-compliance
Lightning Source LLC
Chambersburg PA
CBHW081521040426
42447CB00013B/3299